H.C. Schneidermn

Easter D m October '00

D1061380

THE IDEALS
OF HUMANITY
AND
HOW TO WORK

THOMAS GARRIGUE MASARYK

THE IDEALS
OF HUMANITY

*Translated by W. Preston
Warren*

AND

HOW TO WORK

LECTURES DELIVERED IN 1898 AT
THE UNIVERSITY OF PRAGUE

*Translated by Marie J.
Kohn-Holoček*

*Translation Revised by
H. E. Kennedy*

Essay Index Reprint Series

 BOOKS FOR LIBRARIES PRESS
FREEPORT, NEW YORK

First Published 1938
Reprinted 1969

STANDARD BOOK NUMBER:

8369-1306-X

LIBRARY OF CONGRESS CATALOG CARD NUMBER:

79-90663

PRINTED IN THE UNITED STATES OF AMERICA

CONTENTS

THE IDEALS OF HUMANITY

HOW TO WORK

Part I. Work in General

Part II. Mental, Especially Scientific Work

CONTENTS

9

THE IDEALS OF
HUMANITY

I

INTRODUCTION

Substance of the modern ideal of humanity—
Development of this ideal since the Reformation
and the Renaissance—The ideal of naturalness
and of nature—The religion of humanity—
Differences in the ideal of humanity with
periods and nations: English, French, German;
the Slavs: Russians, Poles, Czechs—Humanity
and nationality—Humanity, the people, and
socialism—Humanity and internationalism—
Cosmopolitanism (liberalism)

THE modern man has a magic slogan: "Humanity," "Humanitarianism," with which he
similarly designates all his hopes and strivings,
just as the man of mediaeval times summed his
up in the word "Christian." This humanitarian
ideal is the foundation of all the aspirations of
our time—especially those that are national. It
is this which is expressed in Kollár's words:
"When you say Slav, may it ever mean man."[1]

This new ethical and social ideal arises
beside the Christian ideal, beginning with

[1] Jan Kollár (1793–1852) was the first of the modern Czech
poets. He interpreted the world significance of Slav regenera-
tion under the influence of Herder's philosophy of nationality.
The quotation is from the inspiring patriotic poem, *Daughter
of Slavia*.

the Renaissance and Reformation. Soon it becomes an anti-Christian and also hyper-Christian conception: *Man*—the idea of humanity, humanitarianism.

This ideal developed gradually. Reason was in part emancipated by the Reformation. A non-ascetic morality came into being; economy and diligence became virtues. At the same time, with the spreading of the knowledge of reading, particularly of the Scriptures, men found energy in the Old Testament. This movement was reinforced by the Renaissance and humanism; these adopted the classical ideal of life, especially the Roman political virtues and their aesthetic views of the universe and life. Science and a new philosophy developed, moreover, and these freed thinking from the authority of the Church.

The State, in modern times, especially the absolutist State, has certainly a great significance. It makes the Church subject to itself, in the sense that it ranks civic virtues higher than Christian virtues. It introduces Roman law into modern social legislation and institutions. The State becomes, with passing time, continually more popular and democratic up to the proclamation of *the rights of men and citizens* in the eighteenth century (with the American and French Revolutions). These rights of man successfully give birth to rights of nationality and of speech, to rights which are social and economic—the right to work and to the necessary minimum for existence— and finally to the *rights of women and of children* (the modern family rights).

Thus the ideal of humanity develops and is incorporated in modern social life.

An essential characteristic of this ideal is that it is represented as natural. Men seek, in fact, the natural bases of religion and theology, of morals and of law—a natural state of society and of the State itself. Philosophy, finally, is based on natural reason (sound judgment and common sense). The new art likewise turns more and more toward nature. The ideal of humanity, in a word, is a natural ideal, a new ideal in opposition to the historic, old one.

This humanitarian tendency manifested itself, more particularly in the nineteenth century, in various attempts to create a religion of humanity (Comte, Feuerbach, and others). In general, moreover, all new philosophies, all new literatures of all peoples, all progressive politics sought to work out and develop the ideal of pure humanity.

This ideal varies with periods and peoples. The English have, to date, worked it out the most comprehensively: philosophically, ethically, socially, and religiously. The French have emphasized its philosophic and literary characteristics. Among the Slavs, the Russians have a religious-social human ideal; the Poles, a national-political one, and we Czechs one of cultural enlightenment. Kollár was for us the herald of pure humanity, as, too, were Šafarik,[1] Palacký[2], Havlíček,[3] and, finally, Augustin Smetana.[4] Kollár, on the basis of the old German philosophy, that of Herder in particular, formulates the ideal of humanity as conceived by the educationist, while Smetana early gave it a social character. Our Czech humanitarianism is the natural development of the ideal of our Bohemian Brotherhood.

The fact that our "awakeners" so strongly stressed the necessity for education in humani-

---

[1] P. J. Šafarik (1795–1861), a great Slavonic scholar, whose work on Slav antiquities, history of Slav literature, and writings on the origins of the Slavs fitted him particularly to be President of the Slav Congress in Prague, 1848.

[2] Frances Palacký (1798–1876), outstanding interpreter of Czech history, who devoted practically his whole life to the history of Bohemia from its beginnings until 1526. He with Havlíček in 1846 framed the Czech political programme and gave the guiding thread of all subsequent Czech policy.

[3] Karel Havlíček (1821–56) accepted Palacký's programme and fought together with him against empty radicalism among the Czechs and absolutism in Vienna.

[4] Augustin Smetana (1814–51), Professor of Philosophy in Prague, who first set "Czech philosophy and thought the task of thinking socially" (Masaryk).

tarian principles may be understood as a reaction to the Catholic counter-Reformation. Enlightenment, culture, education, were the slogans of the people, which thus strove to raise itself from mental and moral darkness. That is why the humanitarian aspirations of German literature in the eighteenth century—which were expressed by Lessing, Schiller, Goethe, and others—spread rapidly in Bohemia and found their warm defender in Kollár.

Art and literature, especially the latter, have a great educative value for the social life of every people. The great masses of people derive from art, particularly from poetry, their ethical and social ideals. Poetry exercises a mighty influence upon life as a whole, upon social and political endeavour. We see this very clearly in the great Polish and Russian poets and also in the influence of Byron.

The idea of humanity in our own day appears as the idea of nationality. We are beginning to realize to-day that the idea of humanity is not opposed to that of nationality—but that nationality, like the individual man, both ought to be and can be human, humanitarian. Humanity is no abstraction enthroned somewhere above real men in the sphere of thought. Nations are, as Herder said, natural sectors of humanity. It is in this sense that Kollár and

Palacký based nationality upon the concept of humanity. Kollár, under Fichte's teaching, worked towards a comprehensive humanitarian national education.

We conceive the idea of humanity and nationality to-day in terms of the people and the community. The people is for us, somewhat different from the nation. "The interests of the people" has become our motto, the ideal toward which our aspirations tend. Socialism in general, like nationality, is an expression of the same ideal of humanity. Before we speak of socialism particularly, however, we wish to touch upon another element in the notion of humanity.

I am thinking here of internationalism and of cosmopolitanism. The idea of humanity implies that all nations have an equal right to strive for their individual rights as a unit of humanity. From this there comes the notion of a world organization embracing all mankind. Practical necessity leads us step by step to this organization. Science, art, economics, capital, and even individual vocations, to-day are internationally organized.

Together with the idea of humanity there has developed not only that of nationality, but also of cosmopolitanism.[1] The Englishman,

---

[1] But there is cosmopolitanism and cosmopolitanism.

the Frenchman, the German, each understands by cosmopolitanism the sovereignty of his own nation and his language. For the smaller and the small nations, though, the situation is quite different. Yet even they cannot remain apart from international organization. With us, Slavonic cosmopolitanism, as Havlíček has very rightly called it, has grown together with the thought of nationality. History teaches that one-sided centralism is injurious on a small as on a great scale, that it must be vitalized through the autonomy of natural economic, cultural, and also national organizations. The older cosmopolitanism, as liberalism formulated it, is giving place to-day to a more adequate development—an uncoerced international organization of independent cultural groups. In this the State recedes before the thought of nationality.

II

SOCIALISM

Ethical tendencies of socialism, Marxism—
Socialism, too, is humanitarian—The "Real
humanism" of Marx and Engels—Economism:
historic or economic materialism—Marxian
amoralism (liberalism)

THE socialistic movement, so far as its final
aim is concerned, is but one of many humanitarian movements. The word socialism signifies essentially the uniting and intimate
association of men. The rights of men were
proclaimed near the end of the eighteenth
century. Liberty, equality, and fraternity were
then demanded in the name of the rights of
man, and they are demanded still to-day. Fraternity—this humanitarian demand is the
basis of socialism. Fraternity, however, can
be variously conceived. Many men are satisfied merely with the words, with humanity
in the abstract. But what is required is to be
a man oneself and to recognize one's neighbour's equal rights as a man. It is for this reason
that men demand political and social rights
in the name of humanity, and it is on this
account that universal suffrage has finally been

20

claimed on grounds of equality and brotherhood. And this is not the only political right
which man demands; there is also the demand
for economic rights, and this demand reveals
the special meaning of the social movement in
our time. On the basis of the political conception of fraternity and equality it is not just
equality in general which is claimed, but
equality which is economic. Thus it is upon
the ground of the idea of humanity which
should be economically put into practice and
not remain abstract, that economic equality
is demanded—fraternity—and fraternity means
communism. Such is the conception of humanity which the socialists of all schools have
formed.

It is obvious that the socialistic notion of
humanity, and communistic humanitarianism,
have altered with the course of time. Even
communism can be quite variously conceived
and executed. Socialism is entirely different
now from what it was fifty and more years
ago. The older socialism which originated in
the last century, in France and England, had
a pre-eminently moral and religious nature.
Such socialism exists still to-day in Christian
Socialism or Christian Democracy (as set forth
in the decree of Pope Leo XIII, 1900).
Parallel with this movement, however, and

coming after it, there is a more economic and political development. This is represented *par excellence* to-day, in all civilized and economically progressive lands, by Marxism and Social Democracy.

This socialism, of which Marx and Engels were the chief founders, derives from the philosophy of Hegel. Hegel's philosophy in the thirties and the forties had an enormous influence on the minds of young people. Feuerbach, who based the ideal of humanity upon religion, was the most important representative of that school. Feuerbach's religion, it is true, was merely a religion of humanity. This (I shall not call it materialistic humanism, but a humanism very closely related to materialism) was the starting-point of Marx and Engels. In their work, *The Holy Family*, they both declare themselves for "real" humanism, by which they designate a humanism which is not utopian.

The basis of Hegelian philosophy is pantheism: the view that the individual, national groups, the whole of humanity and nature, taken together are God. Feuerbach and the radical Hegelians converted this metaphysical pantheism into humanistic pantheism; man became God. They found in man the ideal which the Christian seeks in God. Man was made a deity, but that was not enough for practical socialists like Marx and Engels. They made man a proletarian, and raised this proletarian man to the status of God; more specifically, the whole mass of the proletariat became what God is to the believer.

The basic philosophical doctrine of Marx has been designated as historical materialism; sometimes spoken of as "economic materialism." It is essentially philosophical materialism, atheistic and non-spiritual, the belief that there is no human (immortal) soul. This materialism was propagated vigorously in Europe in the forties and the fifties, and not at all on philosophic but on political grounds. Materialism most frequently is a reaction against a reaction. It gained strength in 1848 when the revolution was suppressed, at the time of the German and Austrian Concordats, and when the reactionary forces particularly in Germany and Austria began to make themselves felt.

The second principle of economic materialism may be defined in Feuerbach's words: "Man is what he eats." Mind, the activity of mind, is a product of the body. The body is maintained by nourishment. The mind, accordingly, is nothing but a product of this nourishment; and since the nourishment is secured by work, the mind finally is the result of work and of production generally. Man then is what he makes. From Hegel's pantheism and Feuerbach's materialistic humanism, Engels and Marx advanced to economic materialism the view that conditions of production (kinds and ways of work, etc.) are the real foundations of all social life, and particularly of all that Marxists recognize as "ideology." The word "ideology" points to a French origin. Napoleon I liked to inveigh against ideologists and to make jests about them, for by ideology he understood a utopianism which is foolish, unreal, unpractical. For Marx and Engels ideology includes philosophy, art, religion, the State, and all that we call the life of the spirit in its broadest sense. None of this, they hold, is real; it is only a "reflex" reflection, or feeble imitation of economic conditions. Economic life alone is real. All history, all development, reduces to the issue of how man can secure food and what generally he may procure for the satisfaction of his bodily needs. Ethics and morals, too, are just ideology. They have no actual significance. And just as Marx and Engels in their later writings placed no weight at all on ethical aspirations and ideals, similarly to-day we very often hear in socialistic gatherings diatribes against "moral ranting," as if all preaching of morals were but a kind of pseudo-ornament of the quite unethical established economic order.

Historic or economic materialism, if thus conceived, tends to further conclusions. The most important is that the proletariat is the real individual and not the individual man, the individual proletarian, and not the proletariat of one nation, but of all humanity. From this comes the international rally-call of Marx: "Proletarians of all lands, unite!" That means: the individual, the personal self, the "ego" has no importance in relation to the mass; as Engels says, the individual is of no importance. Socialism based on this kind of historical materialism is purposely anti-individualistic. That is why the opinion and sometimes the conscience of individuals have no significance for socialists; what is definitely important is the opinion and the conscience of the masses, i.e. the proletarian masses. And since there are far more people in the proletariat than there are capitalists, the interests of mankind and humanity, on the basis of the generally acknowledged principle that the majority vote prevails, are represented by the mass of the proletariat.

One is startled, at first thought, by such flat rejection of the individual. Yet socialism here brings us nothing new. Those who regard the nation and nationality as representing manhood and humanity, as our own humanists do, are also basically opposed to individualism. Political speakers, too, achieve success by inveighing in the name of the nation against individuals and parties; and no one asks them with what, if any, right they are entitled to speak for the nation, or whence they know the opinion of the people about the matter at issue. What, likewise, does the Church signify to its devotees? It is everything; the individual is nothing. We see, accordingly, that this same idea appears in different guises. Nationalism and ecclesiasticalism are also anti-individualistic.

A question arises, however: if the individual has no value whatever, as the collectivists insist, whence then has the mass of individuals its value? If the individual is nothing, if his opinion and conscience are meaningless, wherefore then are thousands of individuals not only something but ultimately all? Here is the exaggeration implied in every formulation of collectivism, but we have to remember that one of the most burning questions of our time is just this conflict between individualism and collectivism, formulated nationally, ecclesiastically, or socially.

The socialists affirm, too, that there is no

morality or code of morals which is valid for all individuals, peoples, and all eras; there is only class morality, since all society rests on the conflict between classes. Each social class, they say, has its own specific morals and its distinctive moral aspirations; the capitalist, the proletarian, the professional man, the workman: each has his own ethics. There is no general morality, they hold, which could unify the rich and poor. This is, I think, sheer exaggeration. There are many classes, it is true, with quite different interests; this no one can deny, any more than that these classes do not love each other particularly. Yet one can say that, in spite of all divergences, there are certain moral principles which are universally recognized. Were this not the case, there never could be any understanding between classes—and it is a matter of concern for them to come to an understanding with each other. It is a fact that men, according as they are rich, comfortable, moderately circumstanced, or impoverished, have their special *mores*, their distinctive manners, which are transmitted from generation to generation, and by which they are differentiated into social classes. It is also true that nations differ in their *mores*. Yet one cannot affirm that they are discordant in essential moral principles—not the Aryan peoples at least. The very history of the concept of humanity shows that this ideal is the common property of all nations. Each has formulated it in his own way, but it is no less true that all possess it. We need to emphasize this fact against all who imagine that humanity, having abandoned the older ethics, especially Christian and ecclesiastical ethics, has disintegrated into lone individuals. This is not true, and for the same reason the teaching of the socialists—that there is only class morality—is not true either.

The Marxists reach an *impasse* through this exaggeration. Their foremost goal is economic equality. The demand for this, however, rests on humanitarian ideals. And if men do not acknowledge these ideals, who then shall effect this equality? And how? Marxists reply: "The State—we do not rely on ethics—the State is to execute the demand for equality." What, though, is the State? To Marxists it is an "ideology" and, therefore, unreal and ineffective. The exaggerated statements of economic materialism involve quite as evident contradictions.

Another question of a still more special nature is: should economic equality be attained by peaceful methods or by revolution? On this question Marx hesitated. Like all radical socialists, he at first advocated revolution. Later he, with Engels, abandoned the idea of revolution and urged the possibility of a peaceful agreement. This question of revolution or reformation, however, is too special for me to treat it here.

We come thus to the final phase of the Marxist movement. The more thoughtful Marxists reject exaggerated economic materialism and approve "ideology" to the extent, I would say, that every intelligent individual accepts it. The "crisis in Marxism" came to an end by ideology, particularly ethical ideology, being finally recognized, and morality and ethical endeavour being acknowledged to be no less real than economic aspirations; in fact, economic striving is ultimately to be understood as ethical. Hence, it comes about that Marxism itself has returned to its old humanitarian programme. I have never doubted that this would occur. Engels and Marx himself never gave up the moral ideal of humanity. Engels indeed is continually preoccupied with morality, a "really human" morality—as he calls it in one place—not just class morality. Bernstein and several of the younger Marxists acknowledge more and more the need for and validity of morality and humanitarianism. The radical socialists themselves, moreover, do not cease to appeal to natural right. What, though, is right? It rests ultimately on ethics and morals, on acknowledgment of the moral code.

I have never made a sccret of the fact that I am a decided opponent of every form of materialism. But I would be unjust if I did not recognize, not the justification of materialism—for that which is wrong never can be justified—but the fact that the one-sidedness of materialism has arisen in opposition to the equally one-sided trend of non-materialism, especially in the Church. I recognize, too, that Marxism has a good influence because its action is not only on the masses, but it compels everyone individually to concern himself earnestly with philosophical and religious questions, besides economic ones. I recognize that it has accustomed us to consider moral questions, questions of moral ideals, better than that mere moralizing which we enjoy so greatly. Early socialism moralized, indeed, too. The school of Saint-Simon, for example, had once quite widespread influence; even in Bohemia. To unite men and strengthen their love the Saint-Simonists had the custom of wearing their coats buttoned behind; they were thus obliged to help each other with the buttoning. There are a great many just such moral games. We all like to sew different kinds of buttons on the backs of our brothers' garments, if possible, so that they can *not* fasten them—Marxism rightly turned against such utopianism and childishness. Inspired by its aversion to such inefficacious morality, it went to the opposite excess: amoralism, I would call it, which leaves morals, which are considered as "ideology," really unconsidered.

With us (in Bohemia) socialism is of older date, though people are but beginning now to realize that socialism exists and what it is. As early as the thirties and the forties of last century there was unrest among workers; the revolution of 1848 had a strongly socialistic element. When our democrats to-day do homage to the barricades of 1848, no one remembers that they were erected by the hands of workmen and defended principally by them. Socialistic *theories* in our country, too, are of older date. Augustin Smetana, whose memory we have recently honoured, was the first to set for Czech philosophy and thought the task of thinking socially. Smetana also, like Marx and Engels, started from Feuerbach; an interesting parallel! Klacel, furthermore, who has been unjustly forgotten, wrote letters on the origin of socialism as early as 1849. In particular, he brought French socialism to us. As for Sabina, he was more anarchistic, especially in the novel *Morana* which he wrote in 1874. Christian socialism began to make its way in the fifties and the sixties, into industrial centres principally, such as Brno and Prague. With us, as elsewhere, socialism was religious in its origin. The origin of Marxist socialism was religious too. Lack of attention to our development is alone responsible for the fact that a considerable part of our intelligentsia has been surprised in recent years by the rapid growth of socialism. Socialism has developed here as in other lands; it could not be otherwise in the land which is the most industrially prosperous of those which made up the former Austro-Hungarian Empire. If we take pride in our industries, we must also reckon with their natural consequence, i.e. with socialism.

I would not wish to produce the impression that my opposition to some theoretic forms of Marxism applies likewise to the workers and the masses of society. Not to recognize the moral power and devotion of the workers would be a great injustice. To condemn entirely the movement of the workers because we do not approve of some of their theoretical views or political deficiencies would be exceedingly one-sided. We have not concerned ourselves about the masses until now, and now we are surprised that they are to some extent organizing against us.

Liberalism, too, has shown, and continues to maintain, a dislike of morality. All liberal theorists, especially economists, who reject morality explicitly and categorically, are and have been teachers of Marxism.

Nor do I wish to state that among us, in Bohemia, there is more morality in the non-socialistic classes. One cannot merely estimate morality by the theories which men hold, and less still by their incomes and taxes.

Our interest in economic questions has grown in these recent years, and since 1848 our slogan has become: *to get rich*. A practical man will not object to this. Yet to be rich cannot be our highest aim in life. What is more important is how people use their wealth. There are men whose sole concern is to be rich, and who become so; they are the slaves of money. Christ said that He was Lord of the Sabbath, and all nations and all individuals should be masters of their riches. That means that we must not permit ourselves to be dominated by materialism, even if it be clothed in the finest phrases of religion or morals, or in any others. It is essential to be master of one's money, to earn it honourably and to use it worthily. In one of Dostoievsky's novels, some young men discuss the problem of economic materialism; some of them have the glowing wish to become Rothschilds. Another of the group, however, says: "Very good, man satisfies his hunger; but what will he do then?" It is as important to consider how one is to utilize one's free time as it is to think of how to get rich. Need compels and example prompts many to work, and it may be said that for the most part they work diligently. Those, however, who attain success find problems awaiting solution; they do not always know how their free time is to be employed. A man who slaves away from morning until night in the factory, writing-room, or library is not dangerous. Danger begins first when there is no work, and it begins even for the satiated. There is also the social and moral problem of unemployment. This is the culminating issue of economic materialism, for in it are summed up all the problems of our nation.

III

INDIVIDUALISM

The substance of individualism in contrast to socialism: subjectivism, individualism, egoism —Aristocratism (literary and artistic)—Liberalism—Anarchism—Nihilism—The individualistic egoism of Stirner—The successors of Stirner, anarchists in literature and politics

WHEN discussing humanism and humanitarianism, I remarked that there are many humanitarian systems. The same is also true of individualism, which is an expression of humanitarian ideals. There are also many individualistic systems.

Individualism is the antithesis of socialism, yet both express the aspirations of humanity. It is thus important not to allow names and opinions to lead us into error, but always to consider the issue itself.

Max Stirner is usually regarded as the philosophical representative of individualism. This philosopher has only become known in recent years, thanks to Nietzscheism and the literary and philosophic moderns. There were in Berlin in the forties several tendencies and schools of liberalistic thought. The most extreme of these was left-wing Hegelianism. As there was then as yet no Parliament in Prussia, the liberal literary parties pursued political aims. The "Freien," Bruno Bauer's circle, which liked to meet in the "Zabbel" tavern, was particularly important during that period. Marx and Engels used to come to their meetings occasionally in 1841-42. Stirner was habitually a welcome guest.

His work, *Der Einzige*, is dedicated to his wife and beloved, Marie Dähnart, who lived in London up to 1898. One of the modern individualists, the anarchistic writer Mackay, who published a biography of Stirner, tried to get some information of him from his wife. But the latter told him little and unwillingly, for they had already parted in anger. It is to the efforts of Mackay, however, that we owe the little that we know of Stirner. His grave remained forgotten until Mackay and Hans Bülow had a new stone erected on it.

Stirner's trend of thought may be summarized as follows: Feuerbach's man and humanity are not satisfying; they are too abstract and unreal. Like Marx and Engels, who desired a real humanity, Stirner wants to take a realistic, wholly non-idealistic, view of man. If I conceive of man realistically, says Stirner, the conflict forthwith ends between what is and what ought to be. It is not man in general who is man; it is I, the absolutely definite individual; I, Max Stirner, I am man. It is what I do, think, feel, which is truly human. This completely specific man, the individual, is the measure of all things. To achieve this realistic view of the ideal of humanity, Stirner demands an entirely different kind of criticism from that which had been used in philosophy to date.

Philosophical criticism up to the present time, although known as critical criticism (so Bruno Bauer, Stirner's friend and later adversary, called it), had been servile criticism, in the service of abstract concepts. We need, however, said Stirner, individual criticism, the criticism of a perfectly specific individual, of an "ego." Only such criticism will be able to displace all "hierarchies," by which term Stirner designates all authority of persons and ideas. If I am the measure of all things, Stirner continues, I am not concerned about anyone or anything. I am the truth; I am the super-truth, he states, and all which seems right to me is right. The right is what I wish and do. Because mankind has been kept up to the present time, in its thought and ideals, in subjection to authority, notably to organized religion, we must above all else abolish this condition. It is not enough, however, to remove the authority of organized religion. We must destroy all thoughts of sanctity. The real aim of Stirner's critique, accordingly, is to un-deify; man must emancipate himself from subjection to phantoms. All general concepts, all religious and political ideals, all ideas even, are for Stirner nothing but phantoms. Thus he interprets the teaching of his master Feuerbach on the anthropomorphic nature of religion.

From this viewpoint it is evident that there is no socio-historical ideal. The history of the State, the Church, the people, means nothing really to the individual. Stirner is, however, somewhat of a Hegelian, and hence he offers a kind of philosophy of history. We can imagine what it is like. He speaks of the past with contempt. Everything up to the present, he holds, is the fruit of illusion. Antiquity is for him an epoch of Negroes. Christianity is Chinese or Mongolian in character, and has the chief demerit of seeking to make men better. The "unique" individual hates all reform. Stirner rejects, accordingly, not only the Greeks, Romans, the Middle Ages, and the Reformation, but he repudiates as well the humanitarian efforts of the present era. Liberalism, in any form, is intolerable to him; particularly political liberalism, because he completely rejects the State. The State is violence toward the individual, and every form of political liberalism tending to reform the State is in principle erroneous. The State, in and for itself, and in general, is worthless. No one should desire its reformation. The notion of reform, at all events, is an expression of the Mongolian or Chinese character of Christianity. Stirner, furthermore, denounces the republic; the republic is a State, and is accordingly no better than an absolute monarchy. The constitutional State alone appeals to him somewhat, because he sees in it the disintegration of the State. Social liberalism, communism, displease Stirner, too, in equal measure, for communists and socialists believe still in the phantoms of society. Society itself is an abstraction—so away with it! Humanitarian or critical liberalism, finally, is no more satisfying. For the "unique" individual, all ultimately amounts to this: to have power and to have it oneself. Power is truth; power precedes and is above right. The individual who acquires and exercises power is perfect. There are no men with failings or sins. We are all perfect.

Such, briefly stated, are the views of Stirner, which we now wish to analyse factually and historically.

I have already said that the philosophy of

Stirner, like that of Marx and Engels, proceeded from Hegelian philosophy and chiefly from left-wing Hegelian philosophy. Feuerbach, and his philosophy of humanity, was the immediate starting-point for both Stirner's anarchism and Marx's socialism. Hegel declared that the universe is God. Feuerbach said: "Man, humanity, is God." Then came the Hegelians of the Left. Marx and Engels proclaimed: "The proletariat, the mass of proletariat, is God." Stirner answered: "No! I am God." Of the pantheistic God of Hegel, Stirner made an individualistic God. The kernel and meaning of all extreme individualism is epitomized in this: "I am God."

To this excessive individualism the radical socialism of Marx and Engels is totally opposed. Engels, in fact, has said: the individual is nothing. Between Marx, Engels, and Stirner a literary argument soon broke out, and since that date socialists have been consistent adversaries of all individualism. Like Marx and Engels, the most outstanding Marxists have always opposed individualism. Only recently, the Russian socialist Plechanov took anarchism frankly to task, on the occasion of several attempted assassinations. Socialists have declared themselves resolutely against active anarchism. Socialism on the one hand, and anarchism on the other, represent to-day the two extremes of the movement toward the ideal of humanity. There is communistic anarchism, it is true, and there are various attempts to reconcile the two extremes, but in essentials they stand in utter opposition to each other.

And now let us try to understand how, besides socialism, individualism has continued to develop from modern ideas. Remember, first of all, that the word "anarchism" signifies the absence of all government, particularly all government by the State, but also all religious, economic, and every other type of administration. (The French philosopher Proudhon, has broadened the meaning of "anarchism.") With the word anarchism the word individualism is quite commonly employed. Fundamentally, the issue is the same.

In the form which Stirner offers it to us, individualism is a purely German philosophic system. I emphasize this point, that it is a German system. The great representatives of modern philosophies in Germany, especially Kant, Fichte, and their successors, were idealists. The word idealism does not denote moral, but philosophic, theoretic idealism, i.e. subjectivism. These idealists regarded ideas as more real than things; the latter had for them a kind of secondary reality, when they were thought to be real at all. What Stirner preached, all German philosophers had taught. German philosophers, I repeat, for elsewhere philosophy had a different nature, less subjective and less individualistic. From this subjectivism Stirner derived his own, mainly moral, views. If, argues he, the subject, I, and nothing else is real, it follows that man, I, should be a total egoist. If man is the measure of all things, he ought to be a thorough egoist.

What, however, is this ego, the "I" of Stirner? Not ideas, he says, but my body is my essential nature. Extreme egoism gives rise thus to materialism. Not mind, not ideas, not ideals: my real ego is my body, and this is the measure of all things. Matter, the body, furthermore, is only satisfied with its own pleasure. It follows that the Stirnerian individual is only to concern himself with what he likes and what is agreeable to him. When self, the body, moreover, is preoccupied entirely with itself, with its own pleasure, Stirnerian egoism becomes sheer nihilism. For that precisely is the meaning of nihilism: apart from my body there is nothing.

The idea of Kant and of German philosophy (as the title of Kant's chief work, *The Critique of Pure Reason*, shows), was criticism. Stirner adopts this element, too, except that he employs in place of criticism in Kant's sense criticism by the "unique individual," which means complete negation of everything outside of the ego-body. This is the second most important characterìstic of the philosophy of anarchism.

Contemporary anarchism has, however, other than Stirnerian elements. First of all comes Positivism; we shall see this later in Nietzsche. Liberalism very often is reproached with being the father of anarchism. In a certain measure this can be maintained, in so far as economic liberalism has against the State, and has desired that it should intervene only negatively in individual affairs, to perform night-watchman service for the rich. Stirner adopted these ideas of economic liberalism; only he went further. It is not just in the economic sphere that the State has nothing to do, he held, but in general; nowhere has it any justification. From the philosophic point of view, also, liberalism can be considered as one element of anarchism.

Later, and especially in recent years—and Stirner had no notion that this would occur—philosophic anarchism gave rise to anarchism of action, to terrorism, and to attacks on persons. This anarchism, when we consider the mass of uneducated anarchists, has a cause which we do not need to search for with a lantern. In Zenker's *About Anarchism*—he is a conservative writer—we find a tabulation of the causes of the development of anarchism among the masses: the injustice of public institutions leads the majority of anarchists to rebellion, without any influence from philosophy. Where greater freedom reigns, it is evident, there is no terroristic anarchism. There is no native anarchism in England, but only foreign anarchists who find a haven there because of political freedom. In France, on the other hand, where even to-day real political liberty does not obtain, and above all in Russia, there are many anarchists. Similarly in Austria there is a good deal of anarchism, though it is not always evident; it is frequently concealed under the name of some kind of socialism.

There is, accordingly, beside philosophic anarchism—theoretical anarchism as it is called —practical political and economic anarchism, the anarchism of action. It is certainly not easy to determine always and everywhere where the anarchism of theory ends and that of action begins. The issue is important and, accordingly, it will be advantageous to examine the character of anarchism still more closely.

Let us take up Stirner's theory again. What is the essential nature of his anarchism?

The followers of Stirner extol him to the skies. Mackay, already mentioned, believed indeed that Stirner's book, *Der Einzige*, would eclipse the Bible and become the gospel of the future. A critical mind cannot subscribe to such extravagance in thought. What Stirner said other philosophers had said before him. Indeed, they had expressed it far more strongly. Stirner's anarchism is not an anarchism of energy, though anyone who does not know well the development of modern thought might take Stirner's view to be original and strong. Considered more closely, this anarchism shows itself to be substantially that of a pedant. There are a great number of such anarchistic Philistines in the world to-day. They are people who denounce everything they can with high-sounding words, but who in reality have no idea of what they are saying. Just such an one was Stirner. To my thinking he is a typical representative of indifferentism. Take Byron and read his *Cain* or *Manfred*: Byron is an anarchist in some sections, too, but what strength and energy there is in him, what resistance, and what revolt against all which he recognized as wrong! In Stirner, on the contrary, there is no trace of battle. It is by his life that he has best shown what pure theory his system is. His *magnum opus* was written in 1845. The rumbling of the revolution was already beginning to be dully heard. It broke out in 1849, but Stirner took no part whatever in it. Our poet Alfred Meissner characterizes Stirner in a reminiscence. (Prague was in close contact then with Berlin and with Germany in general.) Alfred Meissner came to Berlin and brought the manuscript of his epic *Žižka* with him. He submitted it to Stirner, who was everywhere acknowledged as an authority, to read; the latter told the astonished poet that he should not have made a hero of Žižka[1] but a comic character, adding that religious problems had long since gone out of fashion.

Stirner is indifferent to everything; he simply wishes peace and nothing else. He opposes and rejects all that is unpleasant, but he does this merely from the motives of the pedant. That is why he and his theory were totally forgotten; with his book which, to use the popular expression, is nothing out of the ordinary. It is only now, due to Nietzsche's influence, that Stirner has been recollected and has been made a philosophic hero. I do not deny that Stirner is interesting as a representative of German philosophy and especially

---

[1] John Žižka (1376–1424), renowned Hussite general and Bohemian statesman.

because he carried idealistic subjectivism to its extreme absurdity. It is on this account that I insist that his theoretic anarchism is purely a German philosophic doctrine.

The successors of Stirner, for the most part, are also theoretic anarchists. They include, besides Nietzsche—of whom I shall speak later—Mackay, whom I mention once again, and, among the younger writers, Panizza of Munich, who contended with great zeal that Huss and the anarchist Caserio are of equal merit because both sacrificed their lives for their ideas! Next came Hirschberg, who announced with grandiloquence "the right to sin." These anarchists who proclaim in pompous words what everybody long since knows, are quite insignificant in the community; the "right to sin" means nothing more than that every man is weak, that he errs and sins. "The right to sin" sounds like a trumpet call, but there is nothing strong about it.

Beside theoretical anarchism, men often speak of ethical moral anarchism. Tolstoy is considered as the typical exponent of this kind of anarchism. Tolstoy would have no Church, no State, no authority at all. Yet he is an ethical anarchist, since he desires a new morality and a new religion. This same obtains for Ibsen. To avoid error, however, we shall not call Ibsen an anarchist, but an extreme individualist.

People speak also of aristocratism. The word denotes a modern movement which is both literary and artistic. It is found principally in France and is a Parisian tendency, rather decadent.

I now wish to draw particular attention to Russian anarchism. In the Russian politics and literature of the last half-century, anarchism is one of the most burning questions. Bakunin, who was strongly influenced by Prudhon's philosophy, may be regarded as the founder of anarchism in Russia. He was the leader of our "Prague Revolution" in 1848, but Havlíček had already at that time rejected his philosophy and reproached him for his Jesuitism. Bakunin proclaimed, as also did another Russian anarchist, Nietchaiv, that revolution sanctified all means, without exception. It was precisely in this that Havlíček saw, and rightly so, the Jesuitical principle. Terroristic anarchism has spread rapidly in Russia since the appearance of Bakunin and Nietchaiv, and it is for that reason that Russian literature is so urgently concerned with the matter. Anarchism there, following Turgeniev, is called nihilism. The name quite accurately characterizes Russian anarchism. It was used first by Turgeniev in his novel *Fathers and Sons*. Turgeniev was among the first to analyse Russian anarchism. He did so early in the fifties and again later in his *Virgin Lands*. Not only Turgeniev, however, but all the great writers of the country concerned themselves with this problem. Pisemsky, for example, in several of his novels, and Saltykov, Leskov, Gontcharov, Dostoievsky, and Tolstoy. All Dostoievsky's novels, written after his condemnation to Siberian exile, are an analysis of anarchism. It is Dostoievsky who shows best (I must say that he is often unjust) how the absolute ego comes to proclaim itself as God. What, though, is there for this God to do? It cannot create, because such a material, bodily deity is an extremely fragile creature, weak and inept. Nothing remains but to denounce and to destroy; whence, comes revolution and terror. Violence—that is the last resource of this nihilistic deity. "All is permissible" proclaim Dostoievsky's anarchists.

In Czech literature and life, anarchism also plays a part, but in view of our cultural conditions this part is different from that played by anarchism in Germany or Russia. Where anarchism manifests itself among us, though, it has more similarity to German anarchism than to Russian nihilism. Sabina was one of the earliest of Czech anarchists.

D

As early as 1848 he declared his anarchistic ideas. Later he professed nihilism in the novel *Morana*, which I have already mentioned.

Beside political and social anarchism, there is in our more recent literature an individualistic tendency, a kind of aristocratism. This is the German influence once again, the direct influence of Stirner. But it was Nietzsche, above all, who influenced our younger generation. Beside Nietzsche, there were some French writers whose aristocratism was inspired by Renan. Near the end of the eighties came the well-known article of the young writer H. G. Schauer, which was like a proclamation of a national Czech nihilism. This purely national nihilism has continued to haunt us, and there are writers, like Šimaček, who even to-day feel the necessity of defending the Fatherland and the people against it—by means of a purely national appeal, to be sure, without the support of the more fundamental concepts.

Anarchism, call it by whatever name you like, is not Czech. The Czech mind, so far as I can understand the Czech people, will always be primarily social.

I cannot analyse the issue more completely here. Suffice it to point out how numerous are the systems of thought which are presented to us under the names of individualism, subjectivism, anarchism, and nihilism. I hold that all extreme individualism is false in principle, and for the simple reason that no ego exists or can exist alone. Stirner's view is false because of its extravagance. Man is not a God. What kind of supreme Being is he who is born in a family and grows up in a community? Who does not see this? Only theorizing short-sightedness, however profound it may be in appearance, can seek to isolate the individual from all relationships to other individuals. There is no self just in and for itself. Extreme individualism fails morally and theoretically, because it places the human individual on an equality with God.

This is not to say that the efforts of many modern individualists to develop strong in-dividualities are unwarranted. That is a very different matter from the propagation of sheer individualism. Moderate individualism, really philosophic and ethical individualism, desires that in society, by united efforts and on the grounds of love, distinct types, characters, and personalities may be developed.

IV

UTILITARIANISM

Utilitarianism—Ethics of pleasure (hedonism)
and egoism—What specifically is egoism?—English, German, and Russian ethics of utility

UTILITARIANISM signifies the ethics of utility,
of profit (from the Latin *utilis*, useful). The
theory is that usefulness, advantage, ought to
be the goal of every action. On the question
what is it that determines usefulness, we obtain
the answer: pleasure, well-being, happiness.
Utilitarianism then is also hedonism, that is
to say, the ethics of pleasure (from the Greek,
hedone, pleasure). If we ask what type of satisfaction is specifically at issue, we are answered
in two fashions. One group reply: my own
advantage and only my advantage is the object
of my efforts. Others rejoin: not merely my
own gain, but that of the greatest possible
number of people. It is in this sense that people
speak in English philosophical jargon of a
maximum, and a "maximation," of pleasure.
Some go so far that they aspire to the greatest
possible pleasure for all sentient creatures.

The classical land of this philosophy is
England, where Bentham first elaborated it

into a comprehensive system. Every man, said Bentham, naturally strives only for his own pleasure and for avoidance of suffering. I pause here to ask: is it accurate to state that man aspires only to pleasure? Those, for instance, who devote themselves to study and desire to learn something, do they seek pleasure solely, or knowledge? The utilitarian will say that they seek only their own pleasure, for all that men do is but a means to obtaining pleasure. That simply is not true. I do not deny that men do strive for pleasure, but they seek other things as well. The question is whether they strive *only* for pleasure.

A further question is whether it makes any difference what kind of pleasure people seek. Is it a matter of indifference, for example, whether one seeks satisfaction in beer or in a work of art? Bentham here makes no distinction; to him it does not matter what sort of pleasure may be sought. What is important only is that the pleasure be as great as possible, and the more intense it is the greater is its worth. Against this, John Stuart Mill objected that pleasures differ in quality. Mill, I think, is right. He who steals finds pleasure in his stealing. If we acknowledged that every pleasure was in itself good, the world would be in a sorry plight. It must be recognized that all pleasure is not good, but only that which is just and true.

We come here to the greatest difficulty. Bentham held that man is a thorough egoist by nature, that every man seeks pleasure for himself alone. How, though, can such an egoism lead to the utilitarian formula: that the pleasure, well-being, happiness of the greatest possible number of people should be the goal of every action? Whence the consideration for the greatest possible number, if man is a total egoist by nature? How can man come out of himself and enter socially into the interests of his neighbours? This is a difficult dilemma for those who maintain that man is nothing but an egoist, totally devoid of any love for his neighbour, and that what we call the love of our neighbour is but disguised egoism, subtle and refined. Some try to dispose of this difficulty by the assertion that when each finds his own happiness all will be happy. But can one identify "each" with "all"? This might be possible perhaps if each received his happiness direct from heaven and we had no need of others' help, and if it never happened that some men gained their profit through injuring others. How many are there, reputed to be happy, who have secured their happiness by the treading down of others? One cannot say that if each individual is well, all society is well too. If man did not possess at least a little disinterested love for his neighbours, there would be no such thing as society; at all events, society would not be healthy. The weak point of this philosophy—this ethics of pleasure, in brief—is that it denies the innate, disinterested kindliness of men towards each other. Ultra-egoism has rightly been rejected by the critical utilitarians. J. S. Mill went so far indeed as to demand self-sacrifice of the individual.

Utilitarianism spread in England and elsewhere because it appeared to be peculiarly practical. There is no need to reflect long when one is counselled to seek one's own advantage; everyone understands. And yet he only seems to understand. If each man really knew how to become happy, there would not be so much self-caused unhappiness. The motto: seek your own advantage, is not, then, so easy to carry into effect as people have believed. I do not deny, however, that it may be so to a certain extent.

Opponents of utilitarianism have reproached it with being moral trading which may be summed up in the formula: I give to you so that you may give to me. They have called it niggardly, vulgar, and unheroic. If we consider, though, the lives of the founders of this school, we must recognize that they were men of high moral worth. Bentham was consistent in his theoretic egoism. Yet, in spite of that, he worked constantly throughout his life for the common good, and his name is revered throughout the entire world, particularly in England. Desiring to be useful to humanity even after death, he bequeathed his body to the anatomists. As for John Stuart Mill, he was, if that is possible, a man of still nobler character. A small amount of business morality is not so very bad; there is this much good in it that it knows how, and teaches men how to reckon. Most people indeed prefer romantic morality, sentimental philosophy, and ethics; yet if you analyse romanticism and sentimentality you will find that they are still more egotistic than the egoism which is acknowledged honestly and openly.

The representatives of hedonism, avowed followers of Epicurus, are not always given to the coarsest pleasures, or to mere pleasure-seeking. Without speaking of the fact that men quite frequently act better than their theories presuppose, it is a fact that the best of those who have advocated the ethics of pleasure have demanded moderation and sobriety. It may be that this was done by way of egoism and in order not to blunt their sensibility prematurely. Let us not forget, either, that it is the theory of pure egoism, at least among the younger representatives of utilitarianism, which has given rise to social morality. To advocate the advantage of the greatest possible number is to propose to seek the profit of the masses, the majority of the nation, of humanity. That constitutes social ethics. Utilitarianism, in fact, has everywhere given rise to social, and with it socialistic, teaching.

Utilitarianism is the national philosophy of England. The nineteenth century particularly was utilitarian in England, though the beginnings of this doctrine are certainly very much more ancient.

Bentham constructed a system of philosophic thought which in substance is the same as that which Adam Smith and the economists of the last century propagated. English national economy is founded on utilitarianism.

Bentham (1748–1832) was also the founder of the radical-liberal political school. English utilitarianism was a modification of French revolutionary ideas. What the French Revolution wished to accomplish by violence, the English sought to realize by their utilitarianism. The French are radical and revolutionary, the English prudent and calm. The followers of Bentham, like their master, aimed at the democratization of Parliament; they achieved reform of the English Parliament in 1832. Bentham himself, however, was a decided opponent of the ideas of the French revolution and especially of "the rights of man" because they seemed to him to be quite utopian.

The most eminent representatives of utilitarianism, besides Bentham, were the two Mills, especially John Stuart Mill, who reformed utilitarianism and gave it the impress which it bears to-day. Spencer's philosophy of evolution (faith in progress) also accepted utilitarianism. The ethical movement, likewise, which has manifested itself recently in England and America, is essentially utilitarian.

In Germany this doctrine is of later origin. The Germans have had little taste for practical philosophy; they are more utopian than the English. Due to English influence, none the less, utilitarianism gained a foothold here and there in Germany. Feuerbach belongs here, with the utilitarians. From him came Marx and Engels.

Utilitarianism spread widely in Russia. All Russian supporters of empiricism and of the practical socio-political way of thinking were utilitarians. What the Russians called realism was, in principle, utilitarianism. Its most outstanding representatives are the socialistic thinkers and critics Tchernichevsky, Dobroljubov, and Pisarev. This last carried the ideas of Turgeniev's novel, *Fathers and Sons*, to their utmost limit. He declared that all which pleases is good. The practical nature of Pisarev's view led him to fight strenuously against art and aesthetics. What significance has Raphael, he asked? His paintings are not worth a penny. The works of Ruskin, Goethe, Schiller, he judged similarly.

Czech utilitarianism is represented by Karel Havlíček. His philosophy is for the most part utilitarian or, as he himself called it, the philosophy of sound sense. Havlíček lays down no theoretical foundation, but in substance his politics and philosophy are utilitarian.

V

PESSIMISM

Pessimism—The ethics of suffering and the
world's evil—Schopenhauer and his disciples

THE chief representative of modern pessimism
is Schopenhauer. (The word pessimism comes
from the Latin *pessimus*, worst.) The world and
life, according to him, have no value; the
world is the worst of all conceivably possible
worlds. By making this declaration, he placed
himself in opposition to the view of which
Leibniz was the principal advocate, namely
that this is the best of all possible worlds.
Attacking this optimism (from the Latin
optimus, best) he proceeded to reject its philosophical foundation, the belief in God.
Schopenhauer's conviction of the nothingness
of the world and life is therefore atheism, the
view that this world could not be the work of
an all-knowing and perfectly good God.

If the world exists without God, without a
divine creative and directive intelligence, what
then is the essential substance of the world?
Schopenhauer replies: the essential substance
of the world is will. We see the substance of
the will best in the instincts, in the energy with

which these manifest themselves in every creature (most powerfully in creatures which are devoid of reason). The whole world is nothing but will, blind will, blind because the intellect and understanding, in man and in general, is something quite secondary and of little value. Schopenhauer's idea is this: by my understanding, I am conscious of my thought; I reason about myself and the world, but my thought is pure illusion. What is essential in me is will, the will to live. This is the substance of man and everything. Reason is but a sort of lightning flash from the will. Schopenhauer holds—and in that he shows himself, like Stirner, a consistent subjectivist—that matter, the outer world, does not actually exist. It is but the idea of the illusory and illusive reason. (From this, the title of Schopenhauer's chief work: *The World as Will and Idea*.) Man just thinks the world; it does not exist outside his mind. Nothing exists except blind will to live. This will is all; yet this all is really nothing, for the will can and must be broken, renounced. Once reason, in fact, is removed by death, there is no longer any will; there is no reason to have need of it. That is why the substance of the world ultimately is nothing. Schopenhauer's pessimism, accordingly, we see, is nihilism.

Schopenhauer prized art and artistic ideas most highly, for by means of them chiefly, he said, man unveils the mystery of life—that great nothing. Among the arts, music especially was for him *the melody to which the world is set.* Music imitates the world directly, he maintained. That is why it is the primary art. Through Wagner these ideas came to us Czechs also.

If man, now, is convinced, like Schopenhauer, that this world and this life have no meaning and that it is better not to exist than to live, does it not follow that he ought to end his life? There are pessimists, indeed, who advocate suicide. There are even those who would be most willing to advise *all* humanity to make an end of life, if possible at one blow. There were those among Schopenhauer's disciples who did not hesitate to push his theory as far as that. The founder of philosophic pessimism himself gave proof of more discretion by being satisfied at least to live. Schopenhauer formulated on the basis of his pessimism a kind of humanitarian system of ethics, ethics of compassion. Men, he said, are united to each other by compassion; they cannot unite in happiness, for there is none in the world. Schopenhauer strove in the first place to compute the sum of evils; of pleasure there was, for him, no question. If there is some joy, it is but illusory, a diminution of some evil, and hence a relatively lesser evil. The net result is that man ought to quit his life; not by suicide, however, but by resignation. The man who renounces every pleasure is, in Schopenhauer's opinion, a saint. In all religions which are pessimistic, he points out, the saints are objects of great veneration. The saints have rightly seen, in his opinion, that the world is an illusion; they have discerned its vanity and renounced all. The greatest saints are found in India, they are those who of their own choice abstain from all food, thus dominating their wills until, like a candle that goes out, they pass into the eternal nothing (Nirvana). Schopenhauer condemns suicide in perfectly explicit terms: those who try to take their own lives do it in their own interest; they desire something better. Those alone who resign and renounce every pleasure cease to desire anything.

I need not go further into the fallibility of this psychology. It is clear, however, that such a saint has not broken but has strengthened his will. The man who resigns has a stronger will than he who commits suicide—just the contrary of what Schopenhauer teaches. Schopenhauer's whole psychology in general

will not stand the test of careful criticism, and
pessimistic systems collapse when confronted
with life. Pessimists are not consistent.

It is strange, however, that in the nineteenth
century, in an age of progress, during a period
of strong political and economic development,
the philosophy of pessimism could be elaborated
in a highly cultivated nation in the very centre
of philosophic thought. That a pessimistic
philosophy could arise, and that it can still
have so many adherents to-day, is assuredly
a striking sign of the times. It means that our
vaunted progress, our civilization, has more
than one weak point. No person will contest
that Schopenhauer was an outstanding, a
great, thinker. His philosophy, it is true, rests
upon an artificial basis, but all the more
because of that he and his influence are significant if we would judge the times.

This brings us once again to the very bases
of German philosophy. If the "unique" self
alone exists, it cannot be happy. Pessimism
is born of individualism carried to the extreme.
Thus Schopenhauer's chief mood is not de-
spair but anger and wrath. There are other
reasons still why pessimism has been able to
seduce, and still seduces, certain people: for
instance, the predominance which it gives to
emotion over reason. This can readily be

understood. Schopenhauer lived in the era of romanticism; his philosophy is purely romantic. Rousseau had already inveighed against civilization in a romantic manner, desiring man to return to savagery. Schlegel, the German romanticist, later wished man to live like the plants or, rather, to vegetate. Men feared thinking in that period. They fled before it, before the present, to take refuge in the most distant past.

In the second half of the nineteenth century the doctrine of evolution came forward in opposition to pessimism. This was Darwinian at first. Yet it brought faith in progress. For Schopenhauer there was no progress: the world is bad; it may become worse, but never better. In opposition to this view, evolutionism came from England, bringing faith in universal progress. Socialism more particularly accepted this faith; and this has given it its optimistic nature in spite of the elements of pessimism which it still retains. (Socialism, it has been said, is pessimistic for the past and present but optimistic with regard to the future.) It is important that the socialists, and therewith the masses, should have faith that the future will be better. Evolutionism, with its hope, has done more to vanquish pessimism than the newer philosophic systems. Some pessimists,

Hartmann in particular, made the vain attempt to save at least a part of their doctrine by uniting it with evolutionism. Modern evolutionism is the chief enemy of pessimism.

Pessimism has one casual correspondence with utilitarianism. Utilitarianism affirms that each individual pursues his own happiness, his pleasures, and only his pleasures. Pessimism also pursues happiness, but reaches the conclusion that happiness is not accessible.

I, too, think that happiness does not exist, or rather, that it exists no longer for those who set out to find it. Whoever seeks for happiness has already lost it. Everybody likes to be happy; there is no doubt of that. But he who deliberately seeks happiness at any price can no longer find it. This is beautifully expressed in the story of John the Simple. His two intelligent and educated brothers chase happiness, but cannot find it. John the Simple does not think of happiness, but works and helps his neighbours as best he can and lo! he is happy; in the end, he comes to the aid of his unhappy brothers. In this story, our people have given us the greatest moral wisdom: that it is vain to pursue happiness. The conscious and deliberate quest for happiness yields unhappiness. Since the Revolution, modern man appears to be for ever chasing lost happiness, a lost paradise, and that in all domains of life, the economic and the political, in philosophy and in art. Yet the race for happiness renders no one happy.

VI

EVOLUTIONISM

Evolutionism — Naturalistic evolutionism —
Naturalism in general—Naturalistic materialism—Darwinism and its ethics

THE idea of progress has developed in the
modern era parallel with the conception
of humanity. The words progress, evolution,
are familiar to everyone. Formerly, in the
Middle Ages, people did not dream of progress,
I mean collective progress, the progress of
society, the nation, the State. They never had
such a thought. Believing that they possessed
absolute religious truth, men thought that
everything had been eternally achieved. The
possibility of an onward movement, a perfecting
of society, was wholly foreign to them.

Modern times—and precisely because of
this are they modern—are distinguished by
this faith in evolution and progress. This
conception has progressively developed in
different spheres of life. It began with the idea
of progress in science, then in art (the Renaissance), in religion (the Reformation), and,
step by step, in all the domains of thought.

The special name given to this idea of progress is modern evolutionism. Evolutionism means: the doctrine of development. One thinks principally of Darwinism, the theory of Darwin, in this connection.

But Darwinism is to-day only one of many evolutionary theories. Already there are numerous anti-Darwinian evolutionary doctrines. For the most part, however, for most people, Darwinism is synonymous with evolution. I disagree with this idea, but I shall deal with Darwinism because in doing so I can conveniently show what evolutionism means to ethics.

Darwinism rests its faith on progress, on the perfecting and improving of all things and circumstances from generation to generation, upon natural science. It is popularly though inaccurately said that man, according to Darwinism, descends from the monkey. This is the idea—with the doctrine of the struggle for existence—which the vast public have of Darwinism and of evolution. It is by no means right, but in the main it expresses the basic thought of Darwinism well enough.

As for "the struggle for existence," it is a very modern phrase. The word "struggle" is heard everywhere to-day. Darwin thought that every creature fought a constant battle with the others for existence, for its life, and that in this struggle the stronger overcame the weak. The struggle, he maintained, is a means toward perfection. His teaching caught the imagination of the general public because of the way in which it explains the perfecting of society.

Applied solely to animals at first, the doctrine was extended gradually to society, the history of humanity, and to man generally, leading thereby to a great revolution in thinking. Natural science is considered as a great authority, and the interpretation seemed clear. It is incontestable that a struggle exists between individuals as well as between classes and nations. The doctrine of the struggle as a means to progress became familiar to the masses, especially among the social democrats. Everyone will perceive, however, that this theory of struggle is anti-humane. Fighting is not humane. It has been observed, in the first place, that the natural struggle manifests itself in social life in the form of competition. Attention has been drawn to *artificial selection*. Artificial selection is, for instance, seen in military service; the most capable, the healthiest, and the strongest are those who are selected for service, and these are sacrificed upon the battlefield and to the fatigue of military life; the weakest then remain at home and reproduce the human race. A weaker generation accordingly arises. Modern medicine, too, is a means of artificial selection; and it also keeps the feeble alive. Nature destroys the weak, whom human skill endeavours to save, but nature thereby perfects man. Whereas it was formerly believed that man improved on nature, it is the contrary which we hear to-day.

These conclusions on artificial selection and its unfavourable results have led many to declare without circumlocution that the logical consequence of natural selection is the right of the strong to crush the weak. Absolute anti-humanitarianism began therefore to spread. An ethical system which inculcates humanity, it was said, enfeebles men physically and mentally. A new kind of *Faustrecht* (law of the fist) founded upon natural science, was advocated instead. This was proclaimed both for the individual and for nations. The idea of selected nations was proclaimed, not at all in the sense that one speaks of the ancient Hebrews as the chosen people, but of nations selected by nature. Nietzsche particularly has made himself famous by the formula which he derived from Darwinism: "right belongs to the stronger, might is right."

People began to draw other conclusions from Darwinism. Some wished to make

Faustrecht a formula for international relations. Others wanted to correct penal law, contending that humanity protects the criminal and that this protection constitutes artificial selection and a crime against mankind. Criminals are enemies of society, they said, and ought to be severely punished. The ready use of the death penalty is very essential to purify society.

It is comprehensible that, when conclusions like these are drawn, opposition should arise. People became afraid and began to consider what consequences followed logically from Darwinism. Some said: It is not correct to deduce these things with regard to morals and law from the natural 'law of the fist,' for morality is not dependent on theory. I may theoretically proclaim the struggle for existence, but as an individual and in practice accept humanity, Christianity." But that is sophistry. If we are convinced that in all nature, and also in human society, there is this struggle, Nietzsche and his followers are right. Criticisms came from the right and from the left, and gradually the Darwinians came to hold a contrary opinion, namely that evolutionist doctrine had not such radical consequences as had been thought, nay, that it was rather conservative.

I have already said that the Darwinian doc-

trine provoked a revolution in philosophy.
Man is always disposed to think that he is the
centre of the universe, that the entire world exists specifically for him; and now he hears
suddenly that his grandfather, if not his father,
was a monkey. Men adopted this new theory
not because they thought it was scientifically
exact, but because it corresponded to their
revolutionary needs and furnished them with
a weapon for battling with the conservative
reaction. But it became apparent soon that the
Darwinian doctrine was aristocratic, conservative. The socialists accepted the theory of
struggle with a view to furthering their class
struggle. But it gradually came to light that
this theory was not a democratic one. If the
stronger is to survive the weaker, it follows
that the economically stronger, to-day the
capitalists, have the right to dominate the
proletariat. Thus it is that nowadays, not
only aristocratic and conservative, but also
reactionary conclusions are being derived from
Darwinism and evolutionism. Only the *élite*
it is now held, only a small number of more
intelligent and stronger men, have a right
to dominate the mass. Millions and millions
are born so that a small number may survive.
The best-known evolutionists to-day are committed' to aristocratism. Darwin himself was

reserved upon this point. Huxley, Spencer, and others adopted the aristocratic position. Some finally found a way out of the difficulty by saying that while logically aristocratism and Nietzscheism are derivatives of Darwinism, aristocratism is opposed to the innate sentiment of humanity in men. There is, they state, a cleavage between human feelings of humanity, sympathy and neighbourly love, and the feelings operative in nature. These two realms have nothing in common. In the mental, moral sphere the law of love obtains, while nature is the scene of struggle. We must accept struggle as a law of nature, but we must also believe in love and humanity. Love exists to mitigate and refine the rude character of nature's battle. Thus it was that the successors of Darwin, Huxley, Wallace, and others finally make Darwinism humanitarian. The theologians, finally, who had long been enemies of Darwinism, became reconciled. "If God could fashion man from clay," they said, "He could certainly create him from a monkey." Along the entire line this theory, which was originally radical, changed to a conservative and even reactionary doctrine. And this is not the only instance of the bankruptcy of radicalism.

Evolutionism, based on natural history, is not really a new doctrine. It is the ancient faith in progress presented in new form, a historic doctrine scientifically formulated.[1] Ethically the question arises for consideration: what inner motives move men to their scientifically inspired aspirations and strivings? Modern evolutionism can provide no answer to this question. Herbert Spencer, the philosophical representative of evolutionism, reduced his doctrine psychologically and ethically to utilitarianism. The whole mechanism of social life and historical development, according to Spencer, arises from the striving after happiness and pleasure. We meet in evolutionism an old, very old acquaintance.

We are learning more and more that what we have attained—and it is exceedingly imperfect—has developed throughout thousands of years, and that progress is only slowly effected. There are no leaps in history; no miracles will happen.

Such a faith in progress does not contradict the fact that in certain fields there are retrogressions; decadence may occur. Every nation may find itself for a moment at a standstill or in a period of decline. Definitive decadence

[1] The idea of progress is, I think, an established one. Progress does exist; of that, I think, there is no serious doubt. Of course, the idea that there is infinite progress in every direction and that everything will very soon be as perfect as we picture it to ourselves, is utopian.

is even possible, as is demonstrated by the Romans, Greeks, and other nations which have disappeared. We are beginning indeed to-day to conceive of progress far more soberly than we did formerly. We are not losing faith in progress, however; we may say that this faith is justified, however soberly we consider the matter. This faith has something religious in it. If hope in the future is the essence of religion, and if religion strengthens men by inculcating this hope, then evolutionism has a religious nature. Men accept this doctrine exactly as they have accepted, and are accepting, faith in immortality. This is a valuable element in evolutionism.

VII

POSITIVISM

THE word "Positivism" itself indicates the issue. Whoever has heard of positive people, and of positive in contradistinction to negative, can readily conceive that it designates the view by which man instead of breaking his neck in pursuit of high ideals and great eternal truths, limits himself "positively" and practically to reality. Whence this reality? And why? These are questions to which, according to this doctrine, man cannot give an answer. All philosophy, from its beginning to the present, has told us nothing accurate about the origin of the world and life, their causes and their goals. Science can only teach us about what is. Positivism admits that man is also interested in what will be, not at all to satisfy his craving for ideals but to be able to regulate his conduct in accordance with whatever may happen. Positivism desires to lift the veil from the future with the aid of "facts," of "documents." When I know what will occur to-morrow, I shall also know what I ought to do to-day. This, incidentally, is almost all there is to positivism.

Ethically, positivism, as its principal exponents show, is a humanitarian philosophy. Auguste Comte, its founder, proclaimed himself the high-priest of humanity, and established his own humanistic Church. The younger positivists, particularly Taine, were nearer to materialism and, in fact, conceived their doctrine materialistically. Good and evil, virtue and vice, are for them just as natural "products" as sugar and vitriol. It is, therefore, necessary to observe what happens in man and in society and according to this, like a technician, regulate one's conduct.

With all its prevision of the future, positivism has in it a certain element of indetermination. It is surely easy to observe and to foresee, by observing men and history: Greeks, Romans, the Middle Ages, and the modern era. As Musset says: man sits in his arm-chair and looks at the show. It would certainly be highly agreeable thus to contemplate the world and to gather human documents in accordance with Zola's recipe, if only these documents did not concern ourselves.

I too am history. Positivism makes the great mistake that, absorbed in history, in facts and documents, it forgets conscience, as if that were no fact, no document. And in that constant prevision of what will happen,

78

it overlooks the fact that what will be
will be not only of itself, but also thanks to
me, thanks to determination by my will and
conscience.

VIII

NIETZSCHE'S SUPERMAN

I SHALL speak briefly of Nietzsche, as I have already given *en route* everything necessary for the comprehension of his philosophic individuality. Like his idealistic precursors, Nietzsche stresses, above all else, the ego. His view too is individualistic in the extreme. As with Stirner, the *I* is everything: *I*, again *I*, and always *I*. If I alone exist, it is evident that the rest do not exist or else are insignificant. Foremost of all, there is no God. God is dead. That is the new gospel which is preached by Nietzsche. And not only is God dead, but I have slain Him; I am a deicide, and I speak with pride of my titanic act. It is obvious that this world crime has only been committed mentally, but Nietzsche takes pleasure in such strong words. I am more perfect than God, he states. There can be no God, or I would be He; there is no God since I exist. I, Nietzsche continues, I am my body. My body is me. The body is the measure of all things. The body is truth. There is far more wisdom in your body than in your mind or your ideas, or in all philosophy. And what is this body? Nietzsche is not such a crude materialist as to see nothing but matter in the body. No! The body is energy, instinct, will, desire. Instinct is truth; will is truth. The will to be strong, the will to be mighty: such is Nietzsche's formula, derived from Schopenhauer. All morality reduces to the command: Will to be strong! Power, however, has the obligation to create. Whoever has power should create; whoever is mighty must be a creator. And what should he create? The Superman. He who creates ought to be hard. Be hard! This is the new command of Zarathustra. Nietzsche does not reject the love of one's neighbour, but he wishes a new kind of love, hard love. Christianity with its command to love one's neighbours appeared to him servile, weakly, and devoid of energy. The strong man loves, but with a different love. His love is creative and hard.

A second great rule of Nietzsche's is: Laugh, experience the joy of life, a joy which the Greeks knew, but which Christianity destroyed! Nietzsche is in this, too, anti-Christ. "Dance!" says he.

Nietzsche's point of view is decidedly Darwinian: all is permitted to the strong, even violence; truth is revealed in crime. All is permitted to the superman, and likewise, of course, to him who would create him.

Nietzsche wishes, consequently, in opposition to established politics and morals, to effect a revaluation of all prevailing values; he wants to formulate anew everything which has been accepted until now. Nietzsche cannot tolerate the idea of the State as something superior to himself. The State, for him, is an institution for weaklings. The strong, the superman is master of himself and others (anarchism). The nation, likewise, has for Nietzsche no value, in so far as it is organized into a State—whence his fight against the Prussian nation and State. Official nationality is obviously not acceptable to Nietzsche. He conceives of a higher type of nationality, of a nation of masters who feel in themselves their own *Herrennatur*. Such a nation does what it pleases with weaker peoples —does it with blood and iron!

He opposes democracy completely. Democracy and the social democrats seek equality and humanity. Nietzsche demands inequality and despotism. He will have no humanity, but hardness.

Nietzsche, as you have undoubtedly remarked, presents us with no ideas which are distinctly new. Only his methods of expression are new. You find Stirner's view almost letter for letter in Nietzsche's writings. In many a place you find Schopenhauer's philosophy and that of Darwin in all which concerns the struggle for existence and the process of selection. As regards psychological analysis, Nietzsche is greatly indebted to Dostoievsky. His philosophy is fundamentally German. This is seen in his subjectivism, his individualism, and his egoism. Stirner before him had made use of what older philosophers had said.

Nietzsche's favourite word is *superman*. This is clearly just a new way of stating the Darwinian doctrine. I would explain the meaning of superman thus: if man descends from apes (popularly speaking), it follows that in the course of time a yet higher being must arise. As we descend from the apes, the superman will descend from us. Imagine that the superman is now developing in us, and even that he is already here! Wallace, one of the co-founders of Darwinism, believed that we have evidence of the superman already, as he leads and directs us. How, then, does this superman of Wallace manifest himself? In a manner which you would hardly expect: in the phenomena of spiritism. The phenomena of spiritism are thus to be witnesses to the existence of the superman. Man can perceive the superman only as the dumb animals are sensible of man. If now, the superman were already born in us, there would be a peculiar conflict in us, in our consciences:

83

the conscience of the old man in opposition to that of the new superman.

By the superman Nietzsche seeks to save man from decadence. The decline of man accompanies the rising of the superman. Nietzsche seeks, like Schopenhauer (who was inspired in this by Christianity and by Buddhism), for rescue and salvation. There are many others who spend their lives looking for a saviour. Nietzsche's saviour is the superman. And because Nietzsche does not merely trust to biology and nature to provide the superman, but wishes us to create him spiritually in ourselves, he gives very rigorous rules showing us how to rejuvenate ourselves in our progeny, how to make our children healthy and strong. He insists, therefore, on strict chastity. Nietzsche sees decadence everywhere: in literature, philosophy, politics, and in life in general. He perceives decadence even in himself. I do not wish to stress his unhappy end, but I am anxious to point out that his continual calling on the superman and power is not evidence of strength. A strong man would not philosophize about the superman in this way. This is the fallacy in Nietzsche. The strongest words do not constitute power; words do not make a superman. The hard superman of Nietzsche ends, in fact, by feeling just like an ordinary superman, and the superman is only after all a—man. The doctrine of eternal return is not very clear; it is rather difficult to understand; yet it is in fact nothing more than a confession of inability to go further.

Such, briefly stated, is the view of Nietzsche. His doctrine leads us nowhere, for individualism pushed to its extreme is in itself impossible, contrary to nature. I appreciate, accordingly, Nietzsche's confession, for it is for the superman nothing but a confession when he says that individualism and subjectivism lead to a fiasco.

FIRST PRINCIPLES OF THE ETHICS OF HUMANITY

WE have subjected several ethical doctrines to consideration. They are the most important systems tending toward a new, I would almost say a modern, morality. This survey has enabled us at least to note the very large place which morality holds in contemporary thought. Those who reproach our time with a lack of idealism are quite definitely in error. I have no intention of praising our era, but I am anxious to do it justice in this respect.

To conclude, and in concluding not merely to criticize, we shall try to come to an understanding about the most important ethical issues. First of all, it is essential to distinguish between religion and morality. There is a real distinction between them. Morality is not religion, and religion is not morals. Experience reveals that a man can be very reverent, devoted to his Church, respectful of dogmas and commandments, without being moral; he may even be thoroughly immoral. I am not speaking about false devotion. There are so many different forms of religion that simply to think that whoever has a religion is *ipso facto* moral is a mistake. Morality arises from the relationships of man to man; we need morality in our associations with our neighbour. Religion is born of the *rapport* of man with the universe, particularly with God. Religion encompasses a larger sphere than morals; the latter are contained within religion.

Religion ought to be the basis of morality. I cannot conceive of a final solution of moral issues without considering religion. But formal religion, the religion of the existing Churches, does not satisfy me. I wish to have morality founded upon a religious basis, but on that of a religion different from what is officially taught at present. This is not the place to discuss on what religion morality should be based. I shall confine myself to the observation that religion is not to be identified with dogma, the doctrine of the Church. Let us divide, therefore, our religious ethics from these which are ecclesiastical and theological.

When dealing with the fundamentals of morality, one formal question, which is none the less exceedingly important, should be put: How can men know what is good or evil? What determines whether conduct is moral or not? Speaking more concretely, should I derive moral principles from my reason or

87

my emotion? Almost all philosophies of the last century derive the principles of morality from reason. Rationalism characterized the entire eighteenth century. It was the mode then to invoke reason in everything. To-day people like to appeal to emotion both in theory and in practice. Rationalism has been succeeded by an epoch of sentiment. The most outstanding name for the age of rationalism and of ethics based on reason is that of Kant. Pure reason, he maintained, impresses upon man a categorical imperative, an inborn, an inner consciousness of what ought to be; this imperative is sanctioned by reason. Others, on the contrary, say, and I quote only Hume: ethics are not based on reason, but on emotion, innate sympathy, humanity, love. To love one another, that is the law of all morality. There is no need to demonstrate the truth of that law. Emotion expounds it unmistakably to everybody.

I class myself among those who base morality on emotion, but I do not think that emotion ought to be in opposition to the reason. Among feelings there are: good and bad, noble and ignoble, exalted and brutal. Ethics based on sentiment should not lose itself in emotion. I think that the harmony of feeling with reason (and, to some extent, the supremacy of feeling over reason), is the foundation of morality.

Having considered the formal question of how to attain to the fundamentals of morality, we will now attempt to explain these fundamentals. We will choose the best among these which we have reviewed so far, but I greatly fear that it may seem all too obvious. I am reminded here of Eulenspiegel and how he called the tailors together as he had something important to tell them. They all presented themselves only to be admonished never to forget the knots. He who has analysed ethical and philosophical systems and has to reach a conclusion is in a similar position.

The foremost principle of modern ethics, to begin with, is not anything new, but the old and universally acknowledged law: "love thy neighbour as thyself." Who, however, is my neighbour? We speak of the ideal of humanity; I accept this ideal. It has for me a double meaning. It is, first of all, the ideal of proper manhood: to be a man. Secondly, it involves consideration for our fellow humans in the widest sense.

Love of humanity tends readily, however, to become abstract, to exist in fancy rather than in reality. Love needs to be concentrated on specific objects. One cannot love all men equally. We choose and we ought to choose the objects of our love. We need to have some particular objective. To love one's neighbour, if this love is to be efficacious, means to love the person who in point of fact is nearest. To everyone, accordingly, his mother, father, brother, sister, wife, child is his neighbour. We have no idea as yet how much we can do in the narrow circle of those whom we believe we love. Observe yourselves, I ask, and observe others. What is our relation with those who are nearest to us? We would frequently be shocked to discover how little we know them and how slightly we love them in reality. How can we love those whom we know so little? Our children should be the nearest to us of all our neighbours. It has long been written: "Honour thy father and thy mother." It is essential to add, I think: Respect the soul of your child! Think of the coming generations! Let our love be mutual certainly, but let it not be confined to mutuality.

A man's neighbour is his wife; the wife's neighbour is her husband. This very intimate relationship requires devotion in daily life. The wife is fully equal to the husband; only a physical difference may be acknowledged: the wife is weaker.

If the ideal of humanity with respect to

all humanity is too vague, does it become more precise if we apply it to the nation? Is not the idea of a nation still too vague and general? It is a little less indefinite than that of humanity undoubtedly, but for the majority of men the idea of nationality is as abstract as that of humanity. As many falsities have been proffered to us in the name of nationality as in that of humanity.

Love, humanity, must be positive. People often take the hatred of another nation to be love of one's own. It is far higher to feel no hatred, but to love positively. I shall not argue here whether one can love another object as much as that which is one's own; whether, for example, one can love a foreign nation as he loves his own. To require that would be unnatural. To learn to love our own nation, our own family, our own party positively—without an afterthought of hate—will open a whole new moral world to us.

Love must be efficacious. We ought to do something, to work, for our neighbour. Yet excited, noisy bustling and striving is not work; the worker should be calm and conscious of his goal. Work is highly recommended everywhere to-day, but we overlook too much that one can have work even in inactivity. "They also serve who only stand and wait," said Milton.

It is necessary to watch what is happening. Work itself is not the ideal, the final end; it is a means. We shall all confess, if we are sincere, that we like to have as much free time as possible. There is the question, in any case, of what to do with our leisure.

What we call work usually is a matter of small unpleasant tasks which no one likes to do. But we are all romanticists in some measure. We want to be heroes and distinguish ourselves by great exploits. We like heroic deeds, not work. Yet to how many generals, heroes, to how many people is it given to perform great deeds? We all wish to be leaders. There must undoubtedly be leaders, but to be a leader does not mean to be a master or a lord. A good leader is he who knows how to serve, who feels that he himself is led and who wishes to be led. That indeed sometimes requires great sacrifice, though rarely. There are certainly few people who have had occasion to sacrifice their lives. Yet we all picture situations in which we would willingly give our lives for the sake of the "cause." These are only fancies and phrases. What humanity, our family, our party, our comrade needs from us is work.

Let us not find pleasure in martyrdom. We ought not to love death. It is a curious thing how men wish to live yet are not repulsed by death. If one wants to live he should not desire to be a martyr. If we say, "away with torturers!" we must add, "away with martyrs!" As long as there are torturers, there will be martyrs, but so long as there are martyrs, there will also be torturers. Remember that nice Marianne in Turgeniev's novel *Virgin Lands*. She wished to give her life for Russia. She waited constantly for the time to come when the nation would call to her and say, "Now place your head upon the block." The moment never came, but the time did come when Solomin, a practical man, director of a textile factory, arrived and explained to her that Russia awaited no sacrifice of any person's life. What is essential, he explained, is that this dirty child should have its hair combed, that these messy dishes should be washed, and things like that.

To work means to fight ugliness, wickedness, evil, and to fight them constantly. We should fight them everywhere and strive to nip them in the bud. This means nothing radical, only to be persevering and fearless. Fear is the mother of deceit and violence. The tyrant and the deceiver are afraid; he who lives by violence is himself a slave. Seneca has said: *Contemptor suae vitae dominus alienae.* (He who despises his own life is master of the lives of others.)

We ought not to abuse our power; because the world likes to be deceived is no reason for deceiving it.

Love is not sentimentality. We are too sentimental, and sentimentality is egoism. We like to pamper children and also adults, but we have no idea of that conscientious love of which Neruda[1] spoke so true a word. That conscientious love requires that which at first may sound surprising: love yourself too. Yet there is nothing astonishing in that. Jesus has already said: "Love thy neighbour as thyself." But men do not know how to love themselves. Artifice and calculation are not love of self. To love yourself means to take care of yourself. Do not incessantly seek the happiness of others. Do your own duty.

The great evil is that we live continually in concern about what our neighbour will say about us. It is important to have one's own judgment, one's own individuality. We need to resolve to be ourselves and not live on the opinion, the conscience, of others.

Morality is founded on emotion, but not every emotion is just and good. Because morality is based on sentiment, it is not necessarily in opposition to reason. Emotion is blind and

[1] Jan Neruda (1834–91), the founder of modern Czech poetry.

needs illumination by reason. That is why we ought to educate ourselves. Let us have a practical but also general, philosophical training. To-day, too, we especially need a historical and political education. Morality tends to-day to be, to a considerable extent, political. Let us not, then, separate politics and morals.

If we desire education we must be attentive; we must learn to think, but not confuse ourselves by trying to know all. What is important is to attain to wisdom. Not in universal knowledge shall we find happiness!

We need to develop all our powers harmoniously, not merely our powers of mind, but also those of the body. Our education should be as unified and harmonious as is possible.

We should believe in progress. It is essential to believe that the life of the individual and the race can be indefinitely improved. He who believes in progress will not be without impatience. To progress means to overcome what is evil. Yet to conquer evil by good is not very difficult; the difficulty is to supersede good by better.

Man is by nature weak. He is not, however, fundamentally bad. That is why we can, with the co-operation of all, effect progress.

True love rests on hope, the hope of eternal life. Such love alone is true, because the eternal cannot be indifferent to the eternal. Eternity does not just commence with death. Eternity is here now, at this moment and at every moment. We need not, therefore, put anything off to the remoteness of eternity.

In fixing your gaze upon eternity do not despise matter, the body, because of the superiority of mind. There is no matter, there is no body, which is worthless. It is not matter or the body which is the source of evil; it is mind. Impurity is not rooted in matter or in body; it arises from spirit.

Be not idle, but do not permit yourself to become perturbed; for you are eternal. Weigh all with exactitude; what you cannot finish, others will complete. The modern man has no peace or rest. What you do not do to-day you will do to-morrow; what you do not do at all another will accomplish, and if neither you nor anyone does it, then say to yourself that God too cares for what he has created.

The hope in eternal life is, then, the basis of our faith in life. Our faith, I say; for life and work depend on faith. Scepticism, doubt, unfits men for work. But no more can our faith be blind; it must have an adequate foundation. We can only have a faith which has endured the fire of criticism; it must be an established conviction.

Such are the main conclusions I would draw from examination of the several systems of morality. As already stated, they are nothing new. We should not, however, if we wish for a real solution of the mysteries and the problems of life, look for God knows what new revelations. I am continually reminded of the rich young man in the gospels. From childhood onward he obeyed all ten commandments and wished to obtain eternal life. Jesus, however, counselled him, if he would be perfect, to sell all that he had and to follow Him. "No sooner had the young man heard those words than he went away sad, for he had great possessions." I have always pondered the question: was it just because he had to sell his goods that he went away sad? He was obviously a distinctly good young man, educated, and living according to the official standards of religion and morality. Yet he felt the insufficiency of this and on that account he went to the Master in the hope of hearing something new and great. But Jesus gave no other counsel than: *love men!* Let us not seek new or too profound formulae, or mysterious explanations, of the old enigmas of life. These enigmas are old and so also are the solutions. Many of these solutions are good and right. But they will only become right for you, at all events, if you understand them your-

self and apply them to your own life and circumstances. Much that you have already heard
will then acquire new meaning. Thus shall
we go forward, seeing in a new light what we
already know and discovering new aspects of
old things. Depth of thought and penetration
is shown by discerning something new in
what we have long known, in what we hear
every day, in what we have been instructed
about, and were sure we understood perfectly.

HOW TO WORK

PREFACE

IN these lectures I have in mind more particularly ordinary everyday rather than spectacular work, mental rather than physical work.

[handwritten margin note: ordinary everyday work, mental work]

Recently an essay by Tolstoy gave rise to what became a European discussion. It happened this way: Zola, addressing French youth, said that it should cultivate the will to work, for in that lay the salvation of France. Tolstoy contradicted Zola, citing, somewhat paradoxically, the Chinese philosopher Lao-Tse, who declared that inactivity is more beneficial than work, that in inactivity lies the salvation not only of France, but of us all. The constant modern search for work is unhealthy.

These ideas, and especially the situation in Bohemia, serve me as a motive for pointing out the problems hidden here. Both Zola and Tolstoy are right to a certain extent, for Tolstoy does not mean that we should not work at all, but probably believes with Victor Hugo that "A glance at the sky is also an action" and with Turgenev that "A good word is also a deed." But that does not answer the question: What constitutes work, to what extent and how should we work?

PART I

WORK IN GENERAL

1. *Mental and Physical Work*

THOUGH mankind has been thinking of work since the beginning of its existence, it would strangely enough be difficult to find a monograph dealing comprehensively and systematically with the problem of work itself. Economists, for instance, from whom we should most readily have expected it, scarcely enter into the matter at all. This makes one stop and think. It shows that men of learning deal only very late with the most important matters unless they are sensational; though it is almost characteristic of scientific work that it is concerned with the most ordinary things. The scientist studies first what is striking, and work is too commonplace to be philosophized about. Here already we have an indication as to what is work and what is not.

It is only within recent years that people have begun to analyse work as a psycho-physical phenomenon. Usually mental work is spoken of in contradistinction to physical work. The distinction between mind and body was applied to this matter. But the distinction between mental and physical work is as obscure as the relation of mind to body. As soon as we begin to consider the classification of work into mental work and physical work, many difficulties arise. As a rule, a work which entails controlling and administration is regarded as mental. The manager of a factory is placed in contradistinction to the factory hand—the general to the private—the great political dignitaries to the ordinary citizen.

We all consider nowadays that this administrative work is of the greatest importance, we honour it the most. We look upon it as the chief work. This is a rather superficial view, being mainly based on economic considerations. The work of directing, which produces a great and immediate result, is the most highly valued, and rough labour is not highly valued. The thinker in our present-day community is almost as much of a proletarian as a labourer. The mental aristocracy is generally the proletariat. An immediate effect is valued, and in the case of really great and valuable mental work the immediate effect is frequently not forthcoming. Such work bears fruit in future ages. We ourselves are all benefiting from the results of the work of past generations.

What, then, is mental work? If we consider

mental achievement we see two types of phenomenon; on the one hand we have will and
effort, which are regarded as work; on the
other, imagination, which appears to be merely
passive and not to be work. Discrimination,
judgment, seem somewhat more active than
the emotions which are rather passive, subjective. In them, at first sight, there is nothing
active. But even these distinctions are not
sufficient.

By making a distinction between judgment
on the one hand and imagination and emotion
on the other, we treat judgment, imagination,
and emotion as mental material, whereas by
actual work we mean something rather different, such as searching for truth, seeking to
arrive at conclusions. These latter are purposeful and very active. In them we see an aim—
a goal towards which the work tends, which
is its motive power. This purposefulness is a
sign of mental work.

What is physical work?

The term implies the answer: it is chiefly
muscular effort, and physiology declares muscular effort to be the chief manifestation of
life. Besides effort, each muscle generates heat
and electricity. That is work too. Mechanicians
and physicists have a formula for work:
work equals the energy expended multiplied

by the distance traversed. It is significant that this formula originated only in 1826, that it was thus comparatively late when physicists began to consider one of their chief problems. There is much in this matter that is obscure. What gives rise to physical work? Is it the will, or does the law of the conservation of energy apply here?

The question of the relationship between mental and physical work is much more complicated than those just suggested. The chief problem is: Is there absolute parallelism between physical work and mental work? Since there is a certain parallelism between body and mind, the question would arise: Has all mental work its correlation in nervous effort? We do not know. It may be that there are some kinds of mental work, such as comparison, which have no specific physiological counterpart.

Psycho-physical experiments have been made recently with a view to ascertain more exactly the relationship between physical and mental work. These experiments are actually very simple. A man is given something to read, to reckon, or the like, and his respiration, pulse, and temperature are taken. The results of physical labour are similarly measured. When the results are compared coincidences and differences are seen. On the whole, this psycho-physics teaches us nothing; it only confirms what we know in a general way. The experiments only deal with the simplest phenomena, but of course it is better to have our conclusions regarding these more accurately stated. Another method is not to observe the work itself, but rather the fatigue resulting from mental and from physical work. Here, again, we see many analogies and various differences. All these conclusions tend towards the conclusion, which we can also arrive at from common experience, that mental work is accompanied by physical work, and conversely.

It would be important, when we are attempting to find the answer to these questions, to learn which kind of work is fundamental for us. I do not refer to the causal relationship, to the question which work arises from which, I am only concerned with the question whether or not given phenomena are primary in 'Descartes' meaning of the word. I think that the phenomena of mental work are primary in the sense in which the word has been used in philosophy since Descartes' time: that we have not derived conception of work, and, more particularly, of its own purpose, from physical work, but that conceptions grow out of inner experience.

107

When we distinguish between mental and physical work, we shall not always class as mental work what is now popularly conceived to be such; and the same will apply to physical work. The workman sometimes has to think much more than the professor: he has to think how to take hold of some heavy object, how to economize his strength, though of course he does not write a book about it. Nobody would be so bold as to speak of the work of an artisan as purely physical work. The factory hand, too, does much mental work, even if it is only in a negative direction, namely, wishing to do what he may not do; this fatigues him, which shows that it is work; and then he worries about his family and other things. And thus to despise physical work is simply unjust. On the other hand, how is it with so-called mental work? The official, the barrister, the doctor, the judge—is there not as much mechanical work, pattern-work in their routine as in that of a factory hand? A factory is only a model in little of that great factory—the world in which we live. We mechanize everything for ourselves, each of us tries, with all his might, to avoid effort. Deep thought, truth, efficacious work, are by no means guaranteed in members of the so-called intellectual professions. Hence the quarrels between socialism and anti-socialism are based on much misconception.

Thus we really have not muscular work without mental work or mental work without physical work. Only the proportion of each in any given action must vary.

2. *The Origin and Development of Industry as a Human Trait*

Bücher's book (*Arbeit und Rhythmus,* 1896) shows how man has come to work harder and harder. By nature work does not appeal to us. It is distasteful, we earn our bread by the sweat of our brow, perdition itself is based on the idea of toil. Everybody seeks to avoid work, even the most industrious person. Given this native laziness, the problem then arises, how the factory, how scientific studies, how constant work, could all have originated, how man could have become not only a worker, but even a willing one, fond of his task? Bücher explains the matter in this way. It is, he says, an empirically given fact that man in the lowest degrees of civilization is very lazy, and consistently avoids all regular, constant, and hard expansion of effort. But it is likewise a fact that this same indolent individual sometimes takes pleasure in some exciting work, like the dance; he even reaches in it the height of bliss, and pursues it to the point of collapse. How can these two facts tally? The explanation, according to Bücher, is to be found in natural rhythm. This attribute is responsible for the transformation of man from an idle creature into an industrious one. Its presence aids in tasks like hammering and forging metals, rowing a boat, and so forth. The originally lazy man had a natural inborn fondness for rhythm, which he eventually applied to work in general. Physiologically, we have in our bodies various forms of rhythm: the heart-beat, respiration, our gait. Man applies it to muscular activity, and, by secondary association, to work. Bücher refers to the rhythm of motion, not of sound or music. It was only by further association, he says, that man sang as he toiled, that sound rhythm came to accompany work rhythm. Thus we see that primitive humanity associated work, play, and art with each other. He shows how art later separated from the other two; he shows, for example, that various methods of measurement arose from work, and rhythm thus became a principle of economics. What Bücher means by this is that it helps to give us the greatest possible enjoyment and pleasure, at the smallest possible sacrifice of vital strength.

This was soon effected by means of rhythm—work became mechanical, man became industrious. Further, rhythm made work communal. Only with machines, says Bücher, do songs and rhythm cease. Early implements had it, modern machines have it no longer.

This theory, which in my judgment is incorrect, at least makes us realize how man may have become industrious.

I do not believe that primitive man paid great attention to that inborn, physiological rhythm, for it is too slight: we seldom notice such things as the sound of our breathing or the like. The influence, if any, of this natural rhythm was merely secondary. I admit that rhythm is important for work, but in reality it is itself derived from work. Nature makes for periodicity of toil, by divisions into night and day and into seasons. No matter what his task, man is bound to arrive at regularity. Work naturally repeats itself. This fact is of great educational moment, and is of more importance than mere rhythm. Hammering cannot be otherwise than rhythmic, due to its mechanical nature.

If a difficulty is to be overcome by force proceeding from a certain point, it must be exerted periodically: success depends upon the idea behind the strength.

The origin of songs that accompany labour is different from what Bücher would have us believe. Usually, songs are sung only where work permits of singing, just as stories that amuse the working group can be told only where the mind is not fully occupied by the task in hand. It is a certain monotony, a certain boredom, that leads to songs, recitation, and so forth.

Therefore Bücher's explanation as a whole is not valid. He argues that work which is rhythmic saves energy and results in strength. The pleasant feeling of strength is naturally associated with the rhythm that helped to bring it about, and eventually all rhythmic muscular motion is identified with pleasure. Association is thus made the basis of Bücher's theory.

I believe that if rhythm has had any importance, it has only had it as the result of thought, which recognized as rhythmic the periodicity of work; and now the two are identified with one another. Bücher, as is the rule nowadays, underrates early man's power of thought. Even the most primitive of human beings thinks far more than we realize. People on the whole have always been what we are to-day. Primitive man had to apply himself to discover a new method of obtaining what he wanted, even as we do.

I admit that all this is debatable ground. Early man was not concerned with permanent employment—that came later—but with saving his energy. Since work is unpleasant, he wished to do as little as possible, and that is why thought always played a greater role than is generally believed, even in physical work. From what we know, it is apparent that the indolence which characterizes both the savage and ourselves is not a sign of muscular weakness. The savage is physically stronger than we are, and at times works harder; his dance shows his overflowing energy; the primitive negro works more than our labourer, but his work is all to no good purpose. The problem has been and is: not less work, but its rationalization.

We must concern ourselves with mental rather than with physical indolence. The labour of the savage is irregular and to a great extent exciting: he loves the hunt, which not merely brings his muscles into play, but is the staff of his life. That is primitive work. Our concern is the overcoming of a moral, a spiritual obstruction. We wish to make work more methodical, more purposeful. In this rationalization the problem is one of direction, of anticipation, of results, of search for proper means: a mental, not a muscular problem.

Motives for labour were the same in primitive

times as they are to-day. In the first place, there were, and are, the material motives; the natural needs, like hunger and thirst. Hunger is periodic, and induced periodic work. Then there have been the mental stimuli, like greed and ambition. The latter is important. When we labour in public we are more careful. Working in company and competition count for much. Further, like ourselves, our predecessors worked not only for their own persons, but for their dependents. Even the primitive man had a family. Where is the necessity for bringing in rhythm when such impulses as these exist?

Finally, habit has played a part. As soon as a certain work began to be repeated with that natural periodicity, habit would keep it up indefinitely.

Let us not forget these mental and intellectual aspects of work which have been present from the beginning: in these rhythm becomes meaningless, so that Bücher's hypothesis fails.

3. *Romanticism and Everyday Work*

Some of Bücher's conclusions about primitive man, however, are applicable to us all. We are still savages: at least the differences between ourselves and the savage are fairly insignificant. A comparison of our way of life with that of the savage does not come out to our advantage. We see, in the first place, that every one of us to-day still has a distaste for common, everyday, low, unclean work— no matter by what name it is called—and indeed for work of any kind, especially if it be forced and servile, while we enjoy doing what we fancy. We still have Plato's and Aristotle's views on this matter. They too scorned common "low" work. Plato in *The Republic* makes this attitude toward everyday labour the corner-stone of his community life. In this matter, we are all his followers. How is labour spoken of in polite, educated society?

What is a shoe-maker, a clerk? In the public opinion he is a slave. Slavery still exists: we still force ourselves to do "work," that is, ordinary, trifling, low work. Utopians wonder how to get rid of the "vulgar" tasks. Perhaps some will be done away with, others probably not, and new ones will certainly be added. We, in this country, still consider some work "dirty" which in reality is dirty no longer. For us all, manhood begins with a baron, or at least a man who wears gloves. Why go back to primitive man? Let us look at ourselves. We too are fond of exciting labour such as sports and militarism. In industry, gambling on the stock exchange is the type of excitement which modern man seeks. He looks for excitement, too, in the theatre, in politics. While "dirty" work is servile, free work is characterized by various kinds of excitement. Every man likes to risk his life. We find it unpleasant to work quietly, resignedly—we keep on gambling with our lives. Some types of employment offer more of this excitement than do others. This tendency is reflected even in literature, especially in the Russian novel, where people constantly risk their lives and end by committing suicide or murder, but lack the strength for some sedate, useful activity. Pushkin lost his life through this restlessness. There is less gambling in German and English literature—people in those countries are more advanced in this respect. We see it in every aspect of their lives.

It is strange that man loves this game with death. It is strange how death actually lures us. There is a sort of force in it which draws us irresistibly. I can only call it romanticism— which exists not only in literature, but in every field of human action. It did not originate in literature, it merely came there from life, as one special manifestation of life. Of course some ages show more of it than do others; in our century it has been very apparent. To

overcome this romanticism in its bearing on
work is a problem associated with all work.
The savage had to stop dancing and was forced
to learn to work quietly and in co-operation
with others, and so must the modern world.
It depends on us whether we wish to continue
to extend the dominion of death or to raise
ourselves to the level where life and life alone
is paramount, where the goal is not to multiply
deaths, but to maintain life and work to live.

The old tale of Enšpigl is very real: Enšpigl
called the tailors together, promising to reveal
something of vast importance for their craft
to them. When the tailors assembled, expecting
to hear great things, Enšpigl told them to look
out for the knots in their thread.

We all expect something great, gigantic,
something that will attract our eyes and fire
our imaginations. That which seems—and
is—insignificant, does not tempt us. Fancy
always plays a great part in our objectives,
although experience has shown that those
colossal objectives do not even exist.

4. *The Martyrdom Complex*

To sacrifice one's self is to give the greatest
possible proof of the sincerity of one's con-
victions; martyrdom will always remain the

highest proof of moral sincerity. Hence all
nations honour their martyrs. We might say
that society is still organized on the basis
of death. We are impressed with everything
founded on bloodshed, and do not judge
whether it is right, or whether the sacrifice was
necessary. We persecute people to death, and
after they are dead we build shrines to their
memory. What discord between yesterday and
to-day! Nobody can doubt that primarily
young people, who have not much experience
in life, and are only hoping for it in the future,
have a special inclination to spectacular deeds.
There is no question that many a man would
lay down his life for an idea, for his country.
It is a strange fact, however, that when this
same man is asked to give to the same cause—
not his life—but only a few years of hard work,
he does not agree, for he cannot make up his
mind to the heroism of detailed, tedious labour.
If somebody wishing to advise our younger
Czech students said to them: "You need not
drink so much beer, or smoke as many cigarettes
as you do; save your money and give it to your
needy fellow-students. That would be true
brotherly love!"—they would laugh at him.
Why? These young people are not wicked, but
they do not relish petty sacrifices. Ask the
same student body for a big demonstration,

which is really a far worse and more stupid demand, and they will agree. Why? This is in truth a great problem, which demands a solution.

We see already that modern thinkers in increasing numbers have examined this strange tendency of our nature. They advise us to depart from such romanticism. Their views are new, at least they were not much heard in the past. Havlíček and Dostoievsky are among them and William Dean Howells, who says: "Let us try to be able to sacrifice ourselves in little things, to sacrifice ourselves in little things for others. That will be enough. Many a wife who would be willing to die for her husband makes him unhappy by being unable to live for him. Let us not despise the day of small things." Ruskin writes: "The greatest wisdom does not consist in sacrificing oneself; it teaches us rather to find our greatest pleasure in small things."

George Eliot is of the same opinion.

Obviously it is easy to object to these statements. Shall not we become commonplace while busy with all this mean work? Each one of us will pray with Hálek: "From becoming commonplace, oh Lord, deliver me!" Will not triviality become our ideal? Will not insignificance become our prayer? Not at all.

It requires heroism of a high degree to make
petty sacrifices; that is why we avoid them.
And so long as a man does not cleanse himself
from the kind of ethical materialism which
makes him avow them, he cannot estimate
ethical actions at their true value.

Other elements are present in these reactions
of ours: among them a sort of theatricality.
Man wishes to maintain a certain pose, even
in dying. He wants to die in a way which
will make people sit up and take notice. We
all live too much in the minds of others, we are
not sufficiently ourselves. This affects our ambition and our pride. Therefore we ever choose
the spectacular before the unspectacular. Martyrdom in seclusion, martyrdom without show
is very rare. It is natural that the martyr should
wish for the comfort of universal sympathy.
There is nothing evil in such an attitude.
But the other, the quiet sacrifice, is the mightier.
It is important to find in small things the greatness which exists in them. In reality, the
greatness and the pettiness are in ourselves.
He who can derive many sensations from,
and perceive many things in everyday life,
is safe and need not fear becoming commonplace. Under the surface of an outwardly
ordinary life may be hidden emotional and
intellectual depths so extraordinary, that a

man accustomed to showy manifestations has no idea of them. How good to be rich within one's self, and not to depend for wealth on outside activities and the approbation of others!

Furthermore, modern man is almost pathologically high-strung; it may be remarked how acutely he looks for trouble. He finds pleasure in it, he enjoys happiness in unhappiness. Inner peace, no matter how rich, does not suffice him. He looks for painful excitement, for worry. Heine for example shows this tendency when he speaks of Christianity, emphasizing and dogmatically setting before our eyes its sentimental aspects and especially all the martyrdom in it.

Religion and ethics have been reserved too much for holidays. We have little conception of them as applicable in everyday life. Our ethics are for "Sunday" use only—merely "seasonal," just to make an impression on others, not for our own personal use. Real religious feeling that would inspire us at all times, real ethics to guide us in all things—including small ones—are very rare.

If we love our neighbour even as we love ourselves, we will not demand that he should sacrifice himself for our sakes. If we love one another, there must be among us less sacrifice and more work. Let each man help himself first and not impose on others. If we thus rid ourselves of sentimentality, we will simply refuse to make useless sacrifices. For that matter most of this sacrificing that we hear about exists only in fancy, little of it is real. It is often a religious and moral luxury in which we indulge, utopianism, "titanism," mysticism, sentimentalism, and not a strong and healthy feeling.

We are akin to the savage, because we find the idea of everyday work revolting. Ethical romanticism varies in quantity and quality with various ages, nations, classes, and individuals. Peoples on a lower level of development are romantically inclined to dislike work more than are the Western nations. Christianity itself and Christian culture have not yet outgrown this tendency to inactivity, this relic of past times, with its good points as well as its bad ones. Martyrdom has at times played a great role in Christianity. The Church has taken up varying attitudes towards it. The fundamental idea of Christianity—the cult of Christ—is favourable to the evocation of this idea. The crucifix is more powerful than all the dogmatics of scholasticism.

Our century is still to a large extent romantic and painfully sentimental. This makes itself evident, not only in literary romanticism but in all the more important phenomena of the times, such as the tendency to revolution and anarchism. Revolution is the ideal of countless multitudes. Utopianism, aristocratic titanism, are other phenomena of the same kind. Of course the voices of reaction make themselves heard on the other side.

Socialism itself, which began with revolutionary and utopian tendencies, is evolving towards more realistic ends. The labour question is only in recent times becoming a question of labourers, of the heroes of work. The contrast between the old and the new becomes apparent on the one hand: the inclination to avoid work, and on the other hand the *dura necessitas* of working. It is very important for our future development that we should begin to realize that we must outgrow our old inactivity, our innate indolence, and must take a new view of work in general.

The nations vary in their attitude to this matter. We Czechs are somewhat extreme and contradictory. On the one hand we have a predilection for martydom, on the other we are against it. Self-sacrifice has been our ethical ideal since Wenceslaus, St. Ludmila, John of Nepomuk, Huss, and the Unitas Fratrum, through the Counter-Reformation and up to the most recent times. Every politician prates of it. This is a great danger, for the idea of martyrdom will become a commonplace to the nation which toys with it constantly. I am convinced, however, that the very man who exults in it may yet exult in aggressive strength, such as was possessed by the Taborites, by Žižka. Here we see an inborn characteristic of the Czechs: vacillation between the resigned Brethren and the forceful Taborites, between submissive and warlike self-sacrifice. Such vacillation does not lead to constructive determination, as we see in our politics. We fluctuate between radicalism and passiveness. Our greatest men have sought to overcome the tendency to this kind of fluctuation: Chelčický made an effort to unite the Taborite idea with that of the Brethren. It is not that at one time we were softer, at another harder. It is that we lack unity on a higher plane. The Czech "awakeners," Kollár, Havlíček, Palacký, strove for it in as far as they comprehended the problem. And every one of you, who sees that the problem exists, must strive for this higher unity. Here is the chief task for us Czechs: to work against this division, to reconcile the two opposites.

The same contradiction exists in a similar way in other Slavonic peoples. Dostoievsky shows it in many a rare psychological analysis of Russian character; for example, in the person of Dněvnik (the day-labourer), who appears in the story of Vlas. Dostoievsky accurately portrays Dněvnik as a Russian type. He shows that the Russian needs to suffer pain. He shows this also in *The Brothers Karmazov* and in *The Idiot*. He constantly emphasizes the meaning of this need, and how it can be overcome. I believe that Dostoievsky himself yields to this Russian weakness more than he should. Tolstoy is not so sentimental. Kirejevsky compares the Russian and the German in regard to their attitude towards work. The German works systematically, the Russian only when misery stirs him to effort: then he longs to get busy.

The Polish nation shows a mixture of knightly romanticism and the effort to organize the State on the basis of labour.

Thus it is perhaps legitimate to conclude that by nature the Slav has within him a conflict, a contradiction. He who realizes this fact will find his work cut out for him.

The Teutons—especially the Scandinavians and the British rather than the Germans—are more advanced in this respect since their whole life is more based on work than ours, and they are more willing to do ordinary, everyday work than we are. For this reason North America and England are very different indeed from

us as regards the moral regulation of external
life. It is possible that we Slavs do not like
every aspect of their development, just because
we *are* different. Doubtless the English and
the American way has many unpleasant
aspects, for the cult of work is apt to lead
men into certain failings. There is an opposite
extreme to that of romanticism and I hold
no brief for it. Some point out, and justly so,
that it would be a great evil if we became
Americanized. I could find voices among the
greatest English writers preaching against this
extreme devotion to work. Matthew Arnold
constantly censures the Anglo-Saxon for being
too little disposed to meditation, and for having
too great a sense of the practical; nations, he
feels, are directly menaced by becoming too
one-sidedly practical. Morley in his work on
compromise points out the danger to the individual and the nation that sets action above
thought.

Differences in the degree of romanticism
arise with the differences in the training of
various groups, classes, and religions, as might
be expected. Nations may be classified according to religious denomination. The Eastern
Church has long been known to indulge in
contemplation and passivity more than do
Roman Catholicism and Protestantism. It

is characterized by a strange inflexibility, a lack of ability to proselytize; whereas Catholicism and Protestantism are religiously and politically active, Eastern Christendom is passive. It has been taking a more positive stand against the Orient only in recent times. It was shaken from its immobility by the Poles, the Swedes, and the Germans. The Greek Orthodox Church seems dead; but this appearance is deceptive; it shows many signs of life.

Catholicism has been at various times very aggressive, it was the first to organize a Church militant. The whole method of the new post-Reformation Catholicism is active, has a war-like character: discipline, energy, in both the good and the extreme meanings of the terms.

The Protestant sects cater least of all for mysticism; they are rationalistic and dry; they feed the brain. They are well suited to energetic people—merchants, the middle classes. Lecky says that Protestantism is somewhat deficient in heroism and is hard and dry and as specifically practical as coal, which has not unjustly been called the force which made England Protestant.

Class, as has been pointed out, is another cause of differences. We are divided into the "intelligent" class and the working class—two

inimical groups ranged against each other.
There are other differences besides. Journalists,
literary men, artists, are inclined to be "Bohemian." It is customary to associate an uncon-
ventional "bohemian" life with art and genius.
In reality, however, the true artist is only sometimes a "bohemian," oftener he is not: the
greatest artists have not time for this type of
life. Murger in his *Scènes de la vie de Bohême*,
discusses it very well, drawing upon his own
experience. You can see in his work what is
unpleasant in this kind of life. It depends on
loans, it is for the most part a hand-to-mouth,
haphazard existence. And yet, it tempts us
strangely. The romantic element in it is responsible for this. Neruda describes the gipsy life,
with its independence and "liberty." As soon
as we stop to analyse, however, we perceive
that here is not liberty, but rather a struggle
amid the worst possible social conditions,
something low and unattractive. But, indeed,
the artistic community as a whole is "bohemian." Its romanticism, its superstitious ex-
pectation of something great and monumental,
the feeling "Now I shall write an epoch-making
work, now I shall paint a wonderful picture"
—while in reality the artist is in the depths of
want. . . . All this may be reduced to one thing:
the distaste for insignificant unspectacular work.

5. *The Ethical and Metaphysical Significance of Work*

We become people, characters, we become independent only as we work. The idle man is not free, nor is the idle nation. Without work we never have self-confidence enough. With it, we learn our strength. Work is self-knowledge, to know oneself means to work. Whoever does not toil is superstitious, is a beggar, a vagrant, expecting miracles to live by. And since it is impossible to live without effort, the only alternative to working oneself is to enslave another. Thus by labouring we tame our natural violence, and realize love for our neighbour in its stead. Love means work. When moral codes, preaching, and education fail us, work will help. It becomes a balm not only in prisons, but wherever man is to be reformed, in so far as reform is possible. Work shapes the character of individuals, as well as of types and of classes. Sociologists— Comte, Spencer—distinguish between the military and the industrial types. Maurice refers to the knightly and the merchant classes. Doubtless each caste that has been based exclusively on a single kind of work, is one-sided and imperfect. In the scientific world we can trace the effects on character of various kinds of mental work: there is a difference between a naturalist and a philologist, a lawyer and a physician. Individual cases have been analysed by various writers (Macaulay).

A few words should be said about the metaphysical significance of work. Not only man, but every community, indeed all nature, is constantly working. The modern theory of progress and evolution is a theory of work, in the sense that all progress takes place through work, unconscious and conscious. Nature, society, is one huge workshop, but not a completely mechanical or slavish one. Since for us humans work is a means to an end, it is important to know what this end is towards which the nation and all humanity is moving. This end, this ideal, is to be reached by work. A proper understanding of what work is should be the main principle of our general view of life: a view which should be a practical one, a synergism, I should call it, meaning that the co-operation of every one of us may be of constructive value in the evolution of the whole, or on the other hand may retard it or even stop its progress. Man all over the world is a worker. But since work in itself is not the end, but the means, almost the sole means, the question of method becomes a paramount one: How to work? Hence, questions dealing with method, with the skill which enables a man to work well, are the most important, and are not merely put with the idea of using our strength economically. For the very reason that labour is not the goal, we must budget our resources of energy. Even in scientific work, the question of method is the problem of problems.

PART II

MENTAL, ESPECIALLY SCIENTIFIC WORK

6. *Theory and Practice; Motives for Work*

BEFORE we proceed any further, let us clarify the motives urging men to undertake mental work. It has long been said that wonder is what led man to think. The mysteries of the external world and of his inner self are believed to have caused man to philosophize, as though man by nature had a purely theoretical interest in acquiring knowledge. Such a theoretical interest does actually exist, but just how strong is it, and is it naturally strong enough to survive? It is well that there are other and more numerous motives for thought —not so theoretical, but rather of an ethical and emotional nature.

Egoism, self-preservation, ambition, the desire for mastery may be noted among these. We see again that man does not work by his understanding alone, that scientific work is not purely theoretical, but also ethical. Every work has its motive, as valid as the work-for-its-own-sake theory. Some may be exaggerated,

some may seem strange to us, as for example,
Schopenhauer's theory that the intellect is
secondary, that it is the will which counts.
Maine de Biran came to a similar conclusion.
Comte applied it to sociology. Intellect, he
taught, serves only the emotions, which are
the directing forces in man. The emotions thus
control the intellect. The usual way of express-
ing his idea is to say that theory should serve
practice, that theory should serve life, or to put
it somewhat more crudely, that we must eat
first and only philosophize afterwards. To
be sure, add Comte's followers, besides man's
need for food, there are other needs, in the
same category, to be supplied: he must provide
himself with shelter and clothing against the
inclemency of the weather. He has various
instincts: for self-preservation, for reproduction.
The mind merely serves these instincts, these
blind forces, which we cannot understand.
To-day such opinions as these are rather
prevalent and are becoming more and more
popular. Of course, they are not quite correct.
Perhaps the errors of these views may best be
indicated by a quotation from Dostoievsky's
Stripling, in which Versilov holds forth to his
son as follows: "It would be a great idea, to
make bread out of stones—A great idea! But
not the greatest—Man would eat to satiety

and not even say: 'Thank you.' On the contrary, he would forthwith say : 'Now I have had
enough, what shall I do now?' "

To what an extent is pure theory justified and
necessary? Nobody who observes the world as
it is, can doubt the necessity of both theoretical
and practical work. Only the problem of
their proper proportion need trouble us. In
modern warfare, for instance, emotions and the
passions play a great part, but a comparison
between ancient and modern warfare shows that
military science is becoming more and more
theoretical. Courage and blind strength no
longer suffice. The Germans are the most
advanced in this theorization of war tactics,
France and Russia are reforming their armies
on the German model. It is another question
whether the general staff can replace the army
altogether. That it cannot do, but it is none the
less necessary. In modern industry, who could
doubt the need for theory? In recent years the
Germans have, for instance, developed the
chemical industry by devoting themselves in
the first instance to purely theoretical study
of the natural sciences. Such examples teach
us that we need theory a great deal. We still
have too little of it here in Bohemia. Productive
scientific work is all too scant here. Thus it
is madness to preach against theory and scien-

tific work. Of course, the opponents of theory
can always find a ready weapon by using the
word as equivalent to fanciful imagining,
whereas, in reality, exact scientific thinking is
a more appropriate synonym. Another consideration: is everything really practical which
is labelled as such by these supposedly "practical" persons? If it were, a bank would never
fail. Many "practical" people are supremely
impractical. We shall certainly not condemn
theory just because it does not bear immediate
fruit in practice—we do not think for the
moment. Thinking itself would be impossible
without considering the future. Man thinks
further and further ahead. What the ages
invented, we use to-day. The influence of
past generations on ours, the connection of
one generation with another are intellectual.
Hence it is no reproach to say that an idea
cannot be put into practice in a given period.
Of course, we are not to proclaim "science for
science's sake" in imitation of the motto "art
for art's sake," and certainly not "study for
the study's sake"; on the other hand, the
watchword: "Life for life's sake" is too indefinite. What does it mean? Can there be
thought apart from life? If a man must think,
and does so, his thought itself is a manifestation of life. The most that can be asked for

is some kind of harmony between life and thought.

Many who have withstood this exaggeration of the practical, have been led into defending theory, even to the point of fantasy. Victor Hugo distinguishes between the "penseur" and the "songeur"—the one who thinks and the one who more or less dreams. Various quite indefinite ideas, he says, have proved very practical when applied. Certainly it is true that man is not clear in his mind, in spite of all his desire for clarity; there is still going on within us a struggle between darkness and light; intellectually each one of us is naturally confused, and only the practice of a proper method will lead us out of the maze. Let us then distinguish between visible and invisible work, for not everything which is seen is true and real. To be able to make this distinction means to be able to avoid materialism and mechanicalness. I do not deny that nowadays there is a certain tendency in scientific work to be haphazard, a certain weakening of will. Some consider excess of intellectual labour to be responsible for this: an overburdening of the mind. I doubt that all the uncertainty of the world is due to too much theory, but feel that poor theory and imperfect method are to blame. Triflers may want to stop thinking in order to avoid weakening their wills, but I believe that weakness of the will does not derive from too much speculation but rather from an immoral life. All the complaints about theory are exaggerated, especially in our country.

As regards theory, the question arises: What sort of theory? In general, three manners of thought or education may be determined: (1) technical or professional; (2) liberal; and (3) philosophical.

7. *What is the Nature of Scientific Work?*

Above all, it is exact. The very idea of exactitude is derived from this kind of work. The man who does not work scientifically has no *de facto* conception of the true meaning of accuracy, just as the blind man cannot know colours. Usually science is condemned by the very people who understand it least.

What this exactitude is, then, may be expressed only by an analogy. Using this comparative method, scientific accuracy may be likened to the feeling of certainty which people have sought in past times and still seek in a promise given by a man. The oath was the guarantee of security. Scientific work is a constant oath, a ceaseless search for truth and its determination; the consciousness of truth's existence and the ability to prove it when found to be truth—this is the exactitude in question. In science, such accuracy is obtained mainly by means of quantitative evaluation. Qualitative estimation has not yet been successful.

Scientific work is further characterized by observation. To work scientifically means to be observant. Be careful, pay attention, observe closely! There is no other logical rule. Experiment means just simply careful observation, which is not only an intellectual, but also an ethical quality: this quality makes for the diagnosis of truth, for no deception, in scientific matters, of oneself or others.

But constantly, consciously, or unconsciously, we fail to be careful and observant.

This scientific accuracy is influencing social groups more and more widely. While not all people work with scientific precision, they all come into contact with it, indirectly, through applied science, especially through modern technology. For instance, modern railroads have acted as schools for the education of nations, for their accuracy has an influence on the public. Great progress has been made when the masses have learned to measure time, have learned that time is money. Sluggish comfort ceases. Where there are railroads, the people think far more precisely. Keeping to a time schedule is already an achievement, moral as well as intellectual, for it means the keeping of a promise. Here we would observe that in our country we do not bother much about this exactness in "small things."

Our craftsman promises ten times, and does not keep his word. This is not a "small thing"; it may be an accurate expression of the national character or of the character of entire social groups, for it gives an idea of the moral and mental accuracy of the nation or group concerned. Modern factories, modern industry— what educators of society they are! A modern store is something entirely different from an old-fashioned one. The English merchant is as different from the Russian salesman as day is from night. The latter lies and guesses, the former is exact: the price is so much, no more, no less, *do, ut des*. This is an entirely new attitude. Or modern banking provides another example: the repayment of a loan at a time agreed upon is an educational force of considerable significance. What a difference between our school system and the ways that the nature of our civilization forces upon us! There is a vast difference between the requirements of the school and of life. That is the reason why scholastic education does not fit us for reality.

Modern militarism also leads to precision. Thus we all learn exactitude, if not from science, at least from the effects of science.

Scientific work is further characterized by the everyday nature of its subject-matter. The insignificant usually escapes ordinary notice. In former days, investigators occupied themselves with sensational problems, they looked for gold, for the philosopher's stone, for the elixir of life. Now they analyse water, air, the soil, manure, just the objects which are most commonplace, which are all about us, which affect us and enable us to live. Here again, accuracy manifests itself as the observation of neglected commonplace phenomena. The man who thinks scientifically is to be distinguished from the man ignorant of scientific method by the fact that the former finds importance in matters which for the latter hold no interest.

The observation of everyday phenomena is a strain. Objects which are interesting in themselves must inevitably attract attention at least temporarily; those which are uninteresting to everybody require special efforts of concentration.

The third sign of scientific work is its minuteness. The mere fact that it is scientific work shows that it is minute. Induction, its chief aid, is the extremely careful and exact piling up of cases until a generalization is warranted. Somebody is sure to object: "If you understand work thus, what becomes of genius, of great ideas?" This objection is frequently made, but is rather vague. When talking of greatness in this way, people really mean great results. But these often proceed from very trifling causes and forces. And then we must not believe that so-called great ideas are always *de facto* great. Was Newton's idea great? He observed the commonest motions, carried out modest experiments. Nobody can achieve great ends except by beginning with small things. All mighty ideas are marked by an initial attention to matters escaping everybody's notice. The history of each idea teaches us that its emergence was prepared for. Even the greatest thinkers added only a little to the accumulation of the ages. Not to the detriment of genius, therefore, has it been said that genius is an infinite capacity for taking pains, that scientific work means the accurate observation of small details. Geniuses have had the mental and moral force necessary for overcoming the difficulties which beset ordinary human nature. Geniuses have been those who overcame natural indolence.

Accuracy in work is guaranteed nowadays

by organized division of labour. Specialization is more and more practised in all fields of work. At first, this was not so marked. We can imagine how it will extend in the future. Man's attention is capable, of course, of being concentrated within a narrow sphere. The division of labour guarantees progress and many sociologists attribute all progress to it. It is, according to Comte, an essential historical principle, a driving force. A look at a factory convinces us that progress in the field of physical labour is possible only by means of specialization. But it has a parallel importance even in mental labour, for it makes our theories watertight. Without the division of work all of us would have to work harder with our hands to make our own living than we do now.

Specialization, for all the imperfections of our system, still insures to a certain extent a co-ordination of work and talent. Scientific accuracy is the accuracy of the expert. Exactitude without specialization does not exist to-day. Each of us must work through a certain department, must think monographically, must as far as possible avoid constantly roaming throughout the universe. Everybody must strive to be at home in some small corner of this wide world, or he will be a stranger everywhere, and will not penetrate its mysteries. I do not mean that every one of us, especially those who are not taking up science, must write a monograph, but I wish to say that every person, even if he does not wield the pen, can be and should be, a specialist. Let each of us know how to accomplish well at least one type of task, how to read on at least one subject in an accurate, scientific, monographical manner, and not in the superficial, cursory way that so-called all-round education requires.

Even the best things in the world are usually accompanied by evil, and thus even specialization has many a disadvantage. In some ways it does not act: work having been divided, must again be organized into a whole.[1] Extreme specialization does not satisfy us. The accumulation of facts, the addition of detail to detail—these are constantly condemned, and justly so, if the specialized work is nothing more than the piling up of single facts without coordination. We are impelled toward omniscience, we want to know everything, the longing for universal knowledge is instinctive.

Practical necessity, too, drives us to organize. We see this in industry and commerce. Here the faults and errors of specialization are ap-

[1] We see this not only in practical life, and in industry, in trade, in science, too, this organization into a whole is required by logic.

143

parent. Adam Smith points out its effect on the factory worker. The man who is absorbed by only one idea is not only one-sided, but often becomes dangerous, like a man possessed. To conclude, nobody can be an expert in all fields. If work itself, therefore, requires division, and on the other hand our nature and the welfare of society demand its organization, there arises the purely theoretical problem of how we can best get a general education which will help us here.

8. *What is Meant by a General Education?*

To describe it is easier than to tell how it may be obtained. Here the question of method is even more important than in specialized work, for the lack of it here may harm man more. The work must in the first place be classified, and then economically organized.

How should we classify work? There are artificial and natural divisions, and it is necessary to classify all work according to its inherent nature. I will show what I mean by these natural, inherent classes by considering their opposite. Classification is unnatural, when done without regard to the nature of the work itself. For example, when a capitalist unfamiliar with labour organizes a number of labourers, they have no idea what purpose they serve with their work. This is an instance of purely mechanical organization, based on gain. The majority of organizations for work originated from purely practical motives, evolving historically, without any special premeditated theoretical basis. Now we have, *ex post facto*, to correct them.

The social question arises from the endeavour to classify and organize more naturally. It is concerned with science only where no distinction is made between physical and mental work.

Our intellect requires a natural classification and organization of work, which would progress in an orderly way, step by step. General education can only be obtained thus; no sooner do we make a false step, than much of our labour is in vain. If our method is correct, if we proceed not mechanically, but from one sphere to another related to it, thus connecting and consequently simplifying work, making each successive task a consequence of the preceding one, then we may be assured that the consequent economization of energy will help us to secure profound knowledge. That is why the matter of method is so fundamental. The task of proper classification is a task for logic. If our education is thus naturally divided and classified, we shall become clearly aware of our own place in the world and of our environment. This kind of division and ultimate union is so natural that it prevails everywhere, not only in physical work, but in mental, scientific, and artistic work as well. Great artists have frequently been specialists and also capable of work beyond their special branch. (Michelangelo, Wagner.)

What then is a liberal education? It is not a sum-total of information, or a dictionary would be the best educational instrument. People with an encyclopedic store of subject-matter fail to impress us. It is not a sum-total of learning, because knowledge is a living organism. It is we who think and we who work; liberal learning makes a complete human being, or even social group. Therefore, organized, connected knowledge is important. Further, liberal learning is something higher than a single science, for it is not erudition carried to extremes—which is a disadvantage accruing to specialization rather than to general learning. We are now concerned with living, organic knowledge, natural, general knowledge, not with utility.

We do not, however, desire a liberal education which is not accompanied by specialization. Every general scholar should be a specialist in some field as well, for this teaches him accuracy. It is only by specializing that he escapes dilettantism, which usually accompanies generalized study. Specialization is the only remedy for it. All of us are dilettanti to a certain extent, we make use of popular books on various subjects, but let us not deceive ourselves: without proper method, all efforts to achieve a general education are apt to result in but an imperfect, incomplete one. To-day especially, there is the danger of becoming half-educated. A dilettante is a man who confines himself to the title page, to the preface—a superficial person. Dilettantism is not only a mental, but also a moral cancer: it has an adverse influence on character. Education can humanize, but it can also de-humanize; it may be good or bad. It often becomes self-gratification, and is used as a stimulant like strong coffee. The remedy for this evil is a comprehension of the meaning of accuracy and detailed work.

So natural is our longing for general "liberal" education, that all our schools still give it alone. We have not a single specialized school. Specialization thus becomes a matter of self-education. To be sure, even in generalized study self-teaching is necessary, for education does not cease with the school. If schools were better than they are, if they corresponded better with the natural organization of work, they would classify work naturally. In this they fail to-day. In our university divisions, the Faculties evolved throughout many centuries; there is a sort of plan, to be sure, but it is not a great one. Modern Universities are far behind the times, and this is due to this very discrepancy between a natural organization of work and a system of work arranged according to a traditional pattern. This is only a part of a broader social question. The problem of a harmonized organization of secondary schools and universities is a new one.

Journalism is another important medium of education, hence its great responsibility.

General learning is saved from dilettantism not only by specialization, but also by intensified philosophical study. I divide learning into three types: specialized, general, and philosophical. The last-mentioned is something entirely different from the second, for a liberal education is intensified by philosophical study. The liberal gives *multa*, the philosophical gives *multum*.

What is the ethical significance of a liberal education, or of any education?

It is clear that the scholar is qualitatively apart from the specialist. A scholar belongs to a scientific and social category. General learning minimizes egoism, while specialization, by its emphasis on one subject, indirectly increases egoism, for it causes a man to shut himself off from others, it causes a lack of understanding between individuals. Let us imagine a congress of out-and-out specialists: these people could not even talk to each other.

A liberal education is intellectual democracy, a spiritual equality which makes for a spiritual collectivism and community of interest, without which living in harmony with others would be impossible. Individualism must be completed by collectivism. Liberal learning is *eo ipso* humanized and universal, and aims at the union of all thinking and feeling people in. spite of the personal and national differences that may divide them. Herzen says that the humanism of the Russian character is exemplified by the ease with which it can appropriate to itself the fruits of foreign toil. Dostoievsky, speaking of Pushkin, expresses himself similarly, as though the Russian, and to a certain extent the Slav in general, had an inborn capacity for general mental education— for synthesis, for the communism of the mind.

I will touch upon various methods, seemingly trifling and irrelevant, whereby we may now achieve a liberal education. Just as small tasks form real work, so one must come at learning by various unobtrusive indirect ways, which each must learn not to neglect, but to use, like a good husbandman.

9. *How to Read*

A liberal education is gained nowadays more particularly by means of the printed word. The question therefore arises of how to read. I answer—read exactly, scientifically, monographically. I cannot explain these words without giving concrete examples.

In the first place, we must read carefully, in order to grasp all the author's ideas.

Secondly, by careful reading, we must comprehend his method: the manner in which the brain, the spirit of the author works, how he comes to his conclusions, even if he does not describe the process directly.

In the third place, the good reader reads between the lines. Whoever cannot do this will not grasp at all the true significance of a work. By reading an author's work we come to know him. Some authors intentionally reveal themselves as individuals: then the reader's task is easy; but even when we study Newton, we recognize his personality. When we read thus, the book becomes living, and we read with understanding.

To be more specific, I should recommend taking notes. Let each one of us translate some author, attempting to get the spirit of the original. Both Goethe and Tolstoy used to translate. It forces us to read with insight. The practice of making our own index or outline of the work is useful too, seeking to comprehend all its main points. Such reading keeps the mind fit, it is a brain drill. A careful reading of at least one work a year is wise, even though it be only a small treatise.

Is it better to mark books, or not? Possibly each way has its advantages; I believe that writing in the margin is useful in many respects. I recommend the use of a coloured pencil for what is important, a plain lead pencil for what is less so. I have never had unmarked books. In the course of years, I have developed a whole code of special symbols for marginal use.

Another question presents itself: should a whole book or only parts of it be read? This cannot be decided generally : sometimes we read the entire work, at other times a perusal of certain portions is sufficient. As soon as we are sufficiently advanced in a subject, it is well not to read the whole book, but to look up what is relative in it to the idea in which we are interested. By frequent and lengthy reading we acquire a certain technique. The beginner reads much more slowly, not only in the physical sense, but as regards mental grasp, for in due course of time we learn to read a whole idea at a time, rather than single words. We can already tell from the title, the heading of a paragraph, what is dealt with. As we advance in learning, books assume the character of reminders—they only bring to our notice what we know ourselves. When we work, it is well to survey the whole library and look for anything that might be connected with our subject. At a certain age and level of education, we are not concerned so much with single ideas, we aim at a certain completeness, we become apprehensive lest we should overlook something. Books are necessary to this end. My present method of reading is different from my former one. The difference is that now the author points out to me, directs my attention, rather than teaches me.

Too much reading is a fault of our times. The reason for this is the lack of proper method. Reading as an instrument of education has its specific method.

10. *Concerning Books*

From reading we proceed to a consideration of books. We have various instances of what a book can mean to man: what Aristotle's writings, for example, have meant for philosophy, or the Bible, still holy, to all Christendom. A book of course, if it is a good one, is a man; it is more, it is his soul. We can look upon such a good book as upon a letter from a wise man, pleasing, lengthy perhaps, but instructive; to be sure it is a letter only to him who can read. Books are the best of friends. They unite us with the spirits of all nations and all ages. In a well-chosen library we are as in eternity. Here we lose sight of history, we have the oldest and the newest ideas side by side, we comprehend that man is not merely a historical being. Every cultured person should have his own library, personally and altogether his own. Tell me what you read, and I will tell you what you are. We should have books not only as aids to labour, but each one of us should have the works of his own favourite authors; in this realm we can choose our own company better than out in the world. Choose at least one author as your own, and read him very often. The writer who can be read once only lacks quality.

Comparatively poor individuals, possibly even the poorest, may, I believe, each have his own library nowadays. The "educated" person who does not buy books is not really educated. Of course I know very well that people make excuses, saying that out in the country they lack contacts, and so forth. This is not true. Anybody with a little intellectual self-respect, even though he live in a small town, may form a circle which can subscribe for several books. It is a question of a little energy and a little common sense. In England reading has become a national institution.

11. *Concerning Notes*

Each one of us can and must take notes and collect excerpts from the books he reads. We know from experience, however, that these grains of gold are usually lost, unless we know how to organize and file them at once, to form a unit. All of us take notes as we read—the trouble is that we fail to classify them. A good rule is to classify all notes every night or at least every week, that is arrange them according to some definite system. Our education should be a living tree, an integral growth. A fault of the younger generation is the scrappy quality of its thought. It thinks in isolated ideas, not organized into a whole.

12. Concerning Travel

It is important to know how we can educate ourselves by travel, in the country, and in solitude. The opportunity for travel is great nowadays, travel is becoming an important educational medium as well as the school. But I believe that very often we overrate its influence on true education. In the majority of cases travelling is the search for novelties, for what is striking, and only seldom is its goal cultural. I hold no brief against it; indeed, if only from the physical standpoint, for the physicians tell us that it is healthy; I recommend it. I refer only to its educational aspects. Modern nomadism reflects much unrest. Pascal said that all our misfortune is more or less due to our inability to sit still for a while. Kant travelled little, and still he became Kant. To-day it is not necessary to travel to get acquainted with the nation, as we have a quantity of good writings; so that whoever cares to do so, can penetrate into the national life more deeply by study than by travel.

One custom in our country always strikes me: namely, the way in which our people follow the beaten track. Even travel should have a national character, but instead, when the Germans have blazed a trail, we keep on crawling along after them. We constantly hold forth about being Slavs, yet how many of us have travelled through the Slavonic countries? Not even to mention the Balkans and Russia, how many of us are familiar with Moravia, Silesia, or Slovakia?

13. *Town and Country*

A singular view is held by many, namely, that man can educate himself only in the town, which is contrasted with the provinces as a sort of cultural centre. This view is in a large measure correct, and perhaps I over-value or under-value the one or the other. But I notice that the distinction between country and town tends to disappear more and more. Space is nullified by communication: the earth is becoming small, and will continue to become smaller. I cannot, therefore, understand why a man living in the country should have to become rustic and forget everything that he has studied before. What is sought in the town is not to be found there. The town has many faults, for it is an unsystematic storehouse of culture. Many a student in order to pass his examination goes to the country to study. It is not right to use the country as an excuse for backsliding. Even in rural districts and in small towns a group of educated people might be found—clergy, a teacher, farmers, labourers —who would care for a lively discussion and a good book. We still fail in large measure to utilize the various advantages of communication that might be used for education. It is said that the town promotes social contacts. No doubt human associations help us, but they also spoil us. Truly choice, educated company is rare under our conditions, and all of us must more or less fall back upon self-sufficiency. Small groups might be advantageous. We know from history that great movements always had their origin in associations of two or three people. I myself know from experience in club life, that each association lives and is energetic as long as it has no by-laws—that is, while the individuals in it strive hard to have an association, while they have a live interest; as soon as the club acquires a constitution and becomes formal and crystallized, it merely vegetates and declines. A revival will occur only when some of its members acquire active singleness of purpose. A modern mistake is to expect so much of a large organization, which, to be sure, has its advantages, but falls by very reason of its size.

14. *Solitude*

I should like to say a word for solitude and for living within one's self. The man who wants to think must make a bid for isolation, must be something of a hermit. And perhaps the town is exactly where we have more opportunity to think than out in the country. In the city a man can live as in the desert.

15. *Concerning Education in the Universities*

A word as to how we educate ourselves here at the University, that is, as to lectures and their method. The old *dictum* about the living word applies here. But the "living" word may also be dead, it may be excellent, but it may be evil. It is a form, a medium, that may serve a good or a bad purpose.

I do not wish to speak of the schools of Engineering and Medicine; I refer especially to the Faculties of Philosophy and Law. The Faculty of Philosophy is a quite antiquated institution. Universities originated with the ancient Greeks and Romans, and have survived until now. They were perfected during the Middle Ages, under the papal regime, and various reforms have been made from time to time, but, generally speaking, the Universities are an anachronism in the modern environment.

That is why they do not function as we should wish. I see in them the following faults: in the first place, they combine two dissimilar tasks. The University is supposed on the one hand to educate officials, teachers, priests; namely, the professional or practising class. It has, therefore, the function of an academy, a specialized school. Besides, it should and does foster science for its own sake. But obviously this double purpose is not homogeneous, and is not always well served; hence the conflict and lack of unity in our Universities. Neither the one aim nor the other is achieved. Science cannot be freely pursued, nor are the professionals fitly equipped for action. A certain indecision and superficiality result from this disunion. In other lands, for example, especially in England, where they have older institutions, circumstances are different. The English University has these two functions more separated; whoever knows the conditions there will often marvel how well grounded their student is in practical subjects. He knows less theory than a man educated at a German University, but he is not so superficial. It is true that the English themselves are not satisfied with their system and are adapting themselves to the German model. Disunity, which dwells in the spirit of our times, is most patent in Universities.

The second fault of higher education is the manner of lectures. Our University *de facto* does nothing but provide lectures. That in itself is very little, for the manner of giving lectures is obsolete. I often feel that I labour entirely in vain.

The Universities originated at a time when conditions were altogether different, when there were no books. Writing was a tremendous task, a great hardship; the professor did not write books, neither did the student, everything was oral; the professor often followed the works of others. The educational facilities of to-day, books, means of communication—were lacking. What the student did not find out from the professor *ex cathedra*, he did not learn elsewhere. Therefore, the relations between instructor and instructed then and now form a strong contrast. The student body and the professors formed amongst themselves a self-governing community. There was an unbroken transition from student to master and to professor; there was constant association between them, they even lived under a common roof. But as usually happens, we have preserved old forms while environment has changed. We have so many means of education that we can learn differently, we do not need to go to lectures.

The University should be a national and

a social body. How can it be such, when it is an old skeleton without spirit or substance! Lecturing, as it is practised, is unnecessary in many a field: each student should rather be handed a book. This is often only a matter of money: if the State gave every student of philology a good dictionary, the professor would be saved countless quotations; only such lectures would remain as would truly be needed. The professor could lecture only on what interested him and the students. It is a fact that University lectures to-day are not well attended. Would it not be more ethical to recognize this overlapping and to organize a new institution, by utilizing all that is educative, and lecturing only on what holds the attention of the students and supplements their reading and other sources of information? This system would, too, inevitably lead to more thinking. As it is, not only the students, but the professors as well, suffer. I could learn a great deal if I could find out what you are thinking. This would be possible only by closer spiritual contacts.

"Seminars"[1] have been coming into existence in recent times, and these faults have been checked thereby, but only to a very slight

---

[1] A "seminar" is an instruction class, where the students may place their difficulties before the professor or lecturer.

extent. Seminars should have their own period-
icals, rooms, and libraries. The student in
the seminar can learn how to work. In education, just the most important point is method,
learning, how conclusions are arrived at;
the lecture fails to make this apparent to the
young student.

The question arises: to attend or not to
attend lectures? I should answer: attend some,
not others. The more I grew, the more lectures I heard. Especially when one has finished
with lower schooling, he can gain from lectures.
He does not profit at first, because the gym-
nasium (secondary school) and the University
are disconnected from each other.

The third fault is that the student's contact
with the University ceases as soon as he has
passed his examinations. This is not as true
everywhere as in our country. Reform is
needed; higher continuation courses should
be instituted. Teachers, for instance, already
have such courses; all professions would find
them useful. When a man has gained practice
and experience, and has passed beyond
schoolboy worries, a lecture would be useful
both to himself and to the instructor, for both
would learn by it. A plan could be worked out
for instance for courses of a week's duration,
each in a different subject. To be sure, in

our country the situation is abnormal. All of
you who wish to acquire culture, must make
it your task and your duty to be fully conscious
of our insufficiencies and deviations. The
first great anomaly is that we have but one
University and that not a complete one. It
fails, therefore, to meet all our requirements,
various subjects are unrepresented. How we
lag behind other nations in this matter, for
example, Germany, which has twenty-two
Universities! The burden of guilt is not
on us alone, but also on the Vienna Government.

The first concern is, then, that there should
be another University. If we really cared for
cultural achievement more than heretofore,
we should already be speaking of a third one.
A city as rich as Pilsen could found a University for itself, if only it did not care so much
for its beer.

We lack Czech textbooks. Is it not embarras-
sing to me, when I, as an instructor, have to
list sources: Czech ones are non-existent,
so I mention an English title, a French one,
but the student knows neither English nor
French, only German, and I am forced continually to indicate German books! It is a
national lie that we are fighting the Germans—
while we study German texts; it is simply

a scandal that in a Czech University there are not Czech texts. The matter should concern not philosophy, but some business-like publisher.

16. *A Word as to Examinations*

Very often we hear the better students say that examinations are tremendous hardships to them, and frequently a less gifted student makes a better showing in his examination than a more hard-working one. Admitting that in this matter the conditions are different here than in other Universities, I should nevertheless always advise every student to try to dispose of his examinations as soon as possible. They require a certain school technique, and as soon as one has begun to speculate one does not like examinations. It did not hurt even Goethe to be a Doctor of Laws. The idea that an examination would degrade talent is often a sign of rather old-fashioned pseudo-genius, for examinations must inevitably be passed; talented people, particularly, should dispose of such trifles. In our own petty surroundings many a gifted man is struggling for subsistence, is killing himself, just because he lacks qualifications which anybody could acquire.

17. *Concerning the Popularization of Science*

Even in this field we see that conditions are abnormal in our country. We cannot easily speak of University Extension, when we have not even one complete University. Our method of popularization must be special, due to this very peculiarity of our circumstances. Our primary requirement is that our University should become complete, next, that there should follow a second University. Only then the task of arranging for University Extension courses would present itself. We should and could have University Extension, but, as is our custom, we ask our famous Government to get it for us! The Government makes no move, and we also do nothing. Take, for example, Pilsen, which has so many schools, "real" schools (which prepare for the sciences and technical pursuits), gymnasiums (which favour the classics), commercial schools, assuredly there are a hundred professors and teachers there. Could not five be found, who would wish to lecture? Courses could be organized. I have spoken to people from various towns, and they agreed to begin in the summer. I waited and waited; naturally, the courses have not started. These conditions are so, strange, that if one had not so much experience and patience, one would have gone mad.

The main points in all such lectures are:

(*a*) That the themes should be appropriate and practical, and, if theoretical, should be suited to the audience. It is strictly necessary to know the circumstances of the listeners. The theme must be made to their order. An acquaintance with the listeners is essential. That is why in London, and in England generally, the students who lecture to the workers live in their midst in the proletarian neighbourhoods.

(*b*) System is required even in these popular lectures. The lack of such system is an evil, it is wrong that by popularization is understood a sort of skimming of the cream of science: listening to what is interesting, new, peculiar. Thus, superficiality, which is ruinous, is only extended. Even in popular talks the hearer must learn to think, must lose himself in the subject; and even if he himself does not weigh each word, he must feel that thinking is work. The audience must be made to feel that the work is difficult. Each lecturer must decide for himself as to what can be popularized. Geography, History, may be presented in such a manner, that everybody can listen. Some branches of learning do not lend themselves readily to popularization, with others it is altogether impossible, as, for instance, in the case of higher mathematics, Newton's Law. Even if this could be presented in a popular manner, it would always be exact. Therefore, the popularization of science is a far greater problem than most people realize. They think in this country that anybody can do it. Only he, however, who stands at the summit of science is able to fulfil the task properly. How could anybody be a popularizer, who has not himself as yet a complete mastery of the subject?

Thus the popularization of science is perhaps not as difficult elsewhere as here, but we must become accustomed to our own peculiar circumstances.

Another important point would be, in the first instance, to provide a juvenile literature. In the same way that we educate ourselves we should educate our children; we have not yet given this matter thought.

18. *Concerning the Popularization of Art*

Art lends itself more easily to popularization than does science, it is more accessible, it speaks directly to man's heart. Music, poetry, do not require so many commentaries. In this field it is possible to accomplish a great deal, the more so that art aids in scientific work to a far greater extent than we usually realize. It is illusory to believe that science and art are divergent and separated. *De facto* they cohere a great deal; for example, in Bohemia the new novel largely represents and replaces literature in general, including scientific literature. The theatre assumes tremendous importance; it is a great rostrum for general education, a platform from which the masses may be swayed. The point is to provide directive ideas for the masses. All art could be utilized thus. Whoever would like to pursue this thought further should study John Ruskin's works. Ruskin shows how all art in its foundation is of ethical origin, how it can lead to ethical goals, and how it aids learning; he suggests that not only individual dwellings should be beautifully arranged, but that entire cities, and particularly public buildings, should be models of artistry. By such aesthetic work, premeditated to the last detail, the whole nation might be elevated aesthetically and morally, and general education might be spread.

19. *Concerning Self-Education*

Self-education is necessary in greater measure in our country than elsewhere. The objection will be made: why should a young man here especially, have so difficult a task, more difficult than in other countries?

In the first place, I distinguish between self-training and self-education. The former is difficult, but the latter is possible, and we must acquire it, because of our unique situation. And if every small nation, and ours in particular, has a problem, then youth of school age must think about this problem; everybody must make up for his nation's lack of size by well-considered work. The weaker has against the stronger no other resource than to utilize everything whereby he can more or less meet his adversary on that adversary's own ground. Having observed both history and life, I believe that in spite of our smallness we could measure up to many a larger nation, to a great Power, if we but realized our own smallness. An inescapable condition is to comprehend the differences, to grasp what are the causes of this smallness, to remove them, and to utilize our energies more than we have done heretofore.

We have before us a double task: first, we must give each the supplementary information he needs, and which cannot be acquired in the State schools; secondly, taking into account the given conditions, we must attempt to achieve a philosophical synthesis, a union of various conceptions, a general education unified by a single point of approach, a philosophical, complete outlook on the world.

This is something we all lack. Let us imagine a synthesis such as, for instance, the Germans have with their long-standing philosophical leanings and schools with clearly marked traditions, where the individual is led. We keep on starting over and over again, we are only beginning to make history. It is all the more important, therefore, to have a programme and to be able to combine various elements so that an organic whole may result. Our efforts must tend towards the conscious premeditated making of history.

This means that we need to know living foreign languages, if we are to achieve our task in the present-day world. This side of education is apparently formal; an acquaintance with foreign languages is necessary, and I hold that every individual, while he is still in the secondary school, should master at least one, which means that he should be able to enjoy reading it and be able to study in it. We must admit that nowadays with only a knowledge of Czech and without any other linguistic equipment, a general education is an impossibility. To deceive ourselves on this score would be self-deception in connection with the highest aims of life.

Which languages should be studied? Obviously it is beneficial to study primarily the Slavonic tongues, Russian, Polish, and others. They have a vast literature. We Czechs have an added motive for taking up Slavonic philology, namely to be able by the comparative method to comprehend the Slavonic spirit; this is possible only by means of an acquaintance with the original. My experience shows that to learn a Slavonic language, even, for instance, Polish, is harder for a Czech than is generally believed. I might almost say that it is easier to learn Hungarian. The reason is: the more similar two languages are, the more one relies on the construction rather than on a true philological knowledge. One construes constantly, searches out similar words which may have entirely different meanings, or which, perhaps, with the same general meaning, may have different implications. Thus Czechs who can read Russian may miss the exact significance of what they are reading—the Russian spirit is not the same as the Czech spirit; it is quite different and foreign. If we study languages not of the Slavonic group, we have to memorize and thus we learn them, comparatively speaking, better and more easily.

Of course, I should give preference to English. People will study German if only for practical reasons. Comenius of old said that we should study the languages of our neighbours. To-day, surely every educated person knows German. Whether this practice should remain in force is questionable. Our national goal must be to rid ourselves as far as possible of German: not to agitate against it, but to free ourselves from its spirit. That is, our literature and schools must be so ordered that we may be able to acquire a passable general education without even knowing German. Some individuals will always go to the original, but by a thoughtful translation the need for mastering it can be considerably lessened, except for certain groups working at translation. The evil of a universal acquaintance with German is assuredly a threat to us. The only thing to be done is to work against it. Our goal must be to rid ourselves of it all along the line. The matter is not only an intellectual one, but primarily a moral one, for it involves the possession of a certain sincerity, of which we have not enough in this particular case. I know patriots of repute, who are enthusiastic over Slavonic languages, but have not yet mastered the Russian alphabet. They have a great distaste for German, yet send their own sons to German Universities. Such examples are numerous here and we allow it all. Anti-German violence will not mend matters, when combined with a subservience to the German language. The Young Czech party wishes to publish an educational library in which, according to programme, it will print German writings. This signifies a great lack of sincerity. What is at the core of our ethics? We have our national pride only on our lips, yet do not perceive what is worst for our country.

Naturally a liberal education, the learning for which every thoughtful man yearns, must be universal in character. This, however, does not imply roaming around the world, nor a political cosmopolitanism, but rather an understanding of the world from our Czech viewpoint. Goethe said that the world, no matter how large, is after all nothing but the extension of our own being and does not offer us more than our own being. This is true, and holds good especially for us. We shall not reach universality through foreign aid, but must acquire it by our own work; we must make our own affairs the affairs of the world. The Czech nation, the Czech question, must become world-wide; this will happen only through our own efforts. Every man is *glebae adscriptus* (fixed to the soil), everybody will work best where he was born. Many a man is not content at home, but wanders about the earth, seeking contentment Heaven knows where in foreign lands; it is in vain, for he will not find it. Only at home can he work effectively. Everybody is most familiar with his home environment; thus, when our instability ceases, when we concentrate on ourselves here, we shall become acquainted with our own modest qualities and shall learn to make use of them better and to obtain various results. A small nation cannot compete with a large one, but for this very reason we must strive to make our liberal education more national even as we make it broader. To do this would be to show our comprehension of the true Czech spirit and of our history. In short, we must work in order to attain to a truly national culture. The task is fairly difficult, more so here than in countries where the cult of national achievement is being taught in the schools. Since this is not the case here, it becomes the task, especially of the educated classes, to draw upon history, to perceive what is truly Czech, and what is not, and by hard work to acquire what I might call a national education and culture.

Such work, if it is to succeed, in the majority of cases presupposes concerted action, particularly social work for the young people. Perhaps I might contend that work is successful only when it is social, when more persons than one are engaged in it. Work *eo ipso* means that man should aid man; it is *eo ipso* social. The younger, the still inexperienced individual does well to join and work with some tried unit; the student should belong to some corporation or organization; if not to an academic club, then to some other group. So far, our students have joined political parties. Under the circumstances, this is understandable and perhaps necessary, but certainly one-sided. Modern social conditions demand that students should take a far greater interest in social service, which has so far escaped their notice. For example, we have in Bohemia an association the object of which is to re-establish in society the man who has served a prison sentence. The world is hard on such an individual; to put it strongly, society almost forces him to commit further offences. The club helps him "go straight"; in Prague, clubs of this nature are numerous. As far as I know, students have not yet considered taking part in such work. I am certain that as long as there is so little social work here, we shall not advance much. Every younger man benefits by association with a unit the aim of which is good. He profits in two ways;

175

in the first place, such an organization gives him a certain objective, not great enough perhaps to satisfy his fancy, but definite and good. This is wholesome for youthful unsteadiness and vagueness; in the second place, such an association means contacts, it teaches him to work jointly with others. This double advantage is valuable, and therefore it is well for the youth to search out such social tasks.

All this work will, however, have real meaning only if everyone has a definite programme or goal to aim at. Both distant and more immediate objects are necessary. Each action should issue from one's unified view of life, and be its manifestation; thus, not casual, but ordered work is needed.

That is not to say that a man's influence is limited to his conscious efforts. Often one's greatest influence is exerted by those very actions which one does not wish to be noticed, and it is certain that even though a man may have elaborated his plan most carefully, he will affect others more, not only by his spiritual speculations, but also, and perhaps more strongly, by his whole character and his whole life. Every man's life is more influential than his philosophy. The more necessary does it become, however, for him to be careful with his programme, that his character and efforts may be definitely centred. There is no doubt that Victor Hugo was right; our indefinite hopes and ideas are tremendously important. But living constantly in a fog does not suffice; we must give our hopes expression and plan to fulfil them. Our life's accomplishment consists on the one hand in urgent forward effort, which, panting and struggling, we never cease, and on the other in tireless labour, as we work out our life's programme. The two do not exclude each other, and we are always insured against the future when we have a definite plan.

20. *Concerning Social and Political Education*

I shall deal with political education first. Political training is necessary, and becomes more so under our special conditions; in the present-day situation political work is important and may become more so at any given moment. But, as usual, least thought is devoted to the obvious. Though our political tasks are vast, our political training is meagre.

What is meant by political education? Is it possible? Why has it been lacking so far? It has been lacking because the great majority of people do not consider it possible to teach politics. Only very few persons at the present time are truly convinced that even the art of politics may be learned, that even politics require a technical, professional preparation. Comte compares modern politics to medicine in olden times. Politics nowadays are the same sort of mysterious quackery as that out of which scientific medicine grew, and, similarly, politics too must become a science. People have not yet grasped this fact, probably because social phenomena are so tremendously complicated that they cannot easily survey society and its evolution as a whole; therefore while believing in determinism in natural science and in technology, they do not yet admit the possibility of such exact theory being applied to politics.

If politics, then, are a science and a definite profession, what is the chief political problem to be theoretically solved? There is one and only one answer to this question: there is one single political, social, and historical problem: namely, to comprehend the relation of the individual to society, the problem of individualism and collectivism; the explanation of how the individual becomes a social being. As applied in practice, this means a consideration of how the individual should behave towards society, how he may affect the rights and spheres of activity of other individuals.

The problem is, then, to comprehend that both from the theoretical and the practical points of view, man is ζῷον πολιτικόν.[1] It is difficult to analyse the social propensities of man, because our consciousness is purely individualistic and contains nothing collective. We are not concerned with individualism or collectivism as in the economic sphere, but with a noetical, metaphysical question such as: what attributes make the individual a social being, what are his individual and social duties?

How great these problems are, and how much they really imply, may be seen from the way in which the relation of the individual to society has been determined so far. Long ago, all political happenings, all historical events were explained by the direct interference of the Gods. This older notion still prevails. According to it, every action is individual, but this individual action is considered as a manifestation of the whole, which whole is in its turn a manifestation of the divine. We still believe this about the poet, the artistic genius; we consider a prophet an entirely different sort of being from an ordinary man. Great politicians are said to be sent by the mercy of Heaven. Sometimes the aspect of this belief changes, and certain individuals began to regard themselves

[1] A political being.

as a sort of mixture of the human and the divine: courageous warriors and heroes. I believe that this is the popular notion nowadays. A senator considers himself a hero, and every outstanding man, rightly or wrongly, believes himself to be a courageous warrior. Carlyle gave expression to this notion. Quite recently a more democratic point of view has begun to be taken: the whole is emphasized to the detriment of the individual, whose significance recedes before the masses. Such is the approach of socialism and of political liberalism to politics; Tolstoy takes this view in his portrayal of Napoleon in *War and Peace*. In practice, however, even in the masses the individual counts for more than Tolstoy realizes. Tolstoy himself sees a great hero in the "muzhik," and even such individual leaders as Kutuzov assume the same pre-eminent position that heroes once enjoyed.

Thus we see that opinion as to the relation between the individual and the whole is not yet crystallized; the problem is to determine this relation not only psychologically but more especially noetically and ethically. When we seek to explain individual consciousness, we must determine what is individually ours and what is individually not ours, what is derived from the race and what from the species, what makes each of us psychologically a part so to speak of the social organism. Marx says quite definitely that consciousness is not individual, but *eo ipso* collective; hence, that the individual is non-existent. True, this opinion is fundamentally false, but it is consistent.

The logical question arises to what extent does true and right judgment reside in the individual and in the teachings of logic (which is basically individualistic), and to what an extent does it reside in the aggregate? In actual practice the question is solved by the recognition of the majority principle; the judgment of all cannot be determined, and therefore it is approximately defined by the majority of representatives.

Not only is this true in legislature, but more or less everybody subordinates himself to the will of the majority. What is a minority? What is an individual? Rules must be laid down whereby truth may be arrived at. Truth does not depend upon a majority, but is the result of individual work; therefore rights (that is, the rights of the minority) are constantly being defined; therefore the modern legislative task is to establish a franchise which would guarantee the rights of the people as a whole. In addition to the legislature, individual political commissions are at work; they are the means for the utilization of expert specialized knowledge, apart from the opinion of the majority. Further, there is the division of labour between the bureaucracy and the legislature. The latter has not a tenth of the power and privileges of the administrative officials. The real direction of the Government is in the hands of the administrative officials, the legislature acts only indirectly as the supervisor of this machine; hence comes the great practical task of how to reconcile the legislature with the bureaucracy, or in other words, the same old problem of how to harmonize collective opinion with individual expert views.

In the domain of ethics, the question is still the same: how far does right depend on the opinion of the masses? Is the vote of the majority right, or the dictates of the individual conscience? From this conflict proceed the struggles of the individual against the masses, anarchism versus socialism.

Naturally the thoughtful man is faced with the task of a thorough psychological analysis of this relation between the individual and the whole. Individualism is in my opinion far more warranted than collectivism, which would completely destroy individual opinion and conscience; in practice, this latter view is connected with a survival of the old way of looking at

political leaders, as though these had information rarer than that of other mortals. This
point of view constitutes a peculiar political
occultism, superstition, a belief in augury, as
though a representative by being elected, suddenly came to be more than before. It treats
political competence as something not human,
but superhuman. References to the delegate's
superhuman tasks are frequent. Eventually
the delegate himself is infected with this mood
and considers himself a seer and a prophet.
This is a reciprocal mood: he is not more
responsible for it than are the others. The priest
and the physician are regarded in much the
same light. This viewpoint, intruding itself
no matter how sober our judgment may be,
interferes with a proper comprehension of what
constitutes the individual, what the leader.
Leaders there are and will be, but the question
is how should leadership, this outstanding
activity, be judged and evaluated? The position
of leader may be recognized even by democrats, but nothing supernatural should be seen
in it. Then only may the leader be criticized
and the whole group gain. The criticism of
leaders seems destructive to many, and often
well-intentioned people decry it. A widely
held opinion maintains that criticism destroys
the enthusiasm without which achievement

is impossible. Certainly enthusiasm, hope, faith, are important qualities. The man who is only destructive will not build. But everybody recognizes that advancement without education and information is impossible. The question presents itself: how can enthusiasm be preserved without excluding sound and clear reason. Havlíček was an exceptionally enthusiastic man, ready to sacrifice everything, but at the same time he constantly urged criticism and clear thinking and in particular showed that without clarity proper enthusiasm is impossible, for without clarity it will become blind passion, fanaticism. Neruda says that not blind, but enlightened love is right. In our country to-day it may happen, for example, that when criticism of old customs and former generations suddenly gathers force, critics become unjust to the old people, and the old people, on the other hand, cling too firmly to old ways. Progress must be made in accordance with ethical principles. But without clarity proper enthusiasm will be lacking: criticism itself can be enthusiastic. Fervour is opposed by fervour, Reason by reason. Without enthusiasm, even criticism would not be possible. The older men are in the majority, and the majority has all means for persecuting the younger generation. What holds good of the enthusiasm of the old, holds equally good of the enthusiasm of the young. We have no other measuring-rod than logic and again logic. Where criticism is absent, authority rules—and that means the death of all reflection in science and in politics. It is said that an army requires discipline; this is true, but when the army faces the enemy, every officer has his plans in his pockets: during a decisive action he cannot think, he acts. This is the situation in every practical activity. The poet who wished to acquire an education, only when he was about to create, would be making a mistake; he must be educated already, he must stand on the crest of the wave, he must know the leading tendencies of the times. As soon as he begins to create he forgets self and life.

All enthusiastic work has similar characteristics, whatever its scope. Sound preliminary education is needed, not a summary collection of information. The whole man must be educated, formed by his education; later, in practice, this will reveal itself. To-day, when the State assumes more and more activities, when it becomes something fundamentally different from what it was formerly, from the absolutist State, political activity becomes more varied. Therefore it is necessary to give thought to the utilization of everything possible in order to attain the political goal. We think only of legislative, parliamentary activity as political. This is a mistake. Everybody can be politically active, be he teacher, physician, or architect, if he is rightly active in his own field—that is, if only he works well.

Besides this political work in the broader sense, political work in the more specific sense is necessary. Every educated person should teach the people and should school himself. The contact of every individual with the masses is beneficial to him. I do not know how candidates can stand before their electors and give them advice and at the same time be unwilling to learn from them; the point is, they do not know how to learn from them. Of course if the expert wanted to learn expertness from the people, he would be lost; he must be able to say to them that they do not understand this or that. But everybody who lives with the people may learn much. It is possible to learn from the most insignificant man; one word, one gesture may be instructive. But such profitable learning presupposes a certain love for the masses—a love which is not economic. The educated classes do not live with the masses. If they did, there would be much mutual instruction.

Political activity, whether in the broader

or in the narrower sense, does not mean activity in political parties only, but, outside party, anywhere. It is possible to work everywhere, wherever one happens to be and wherever one goes, for one's own self and for the whole.

One thing especially should be clear to our politically educated classes, namely, that everywhere, in all parts of our Czech country, people should understand each other, even if they are not formally united by party or caste, that there should be among them a *tacitus consensus*. The nation lacking such accord is in a bad way. Every nation, sect, State, society, or organization is lost if it has no members who understand each other without explanations. Why cannot a person in Prague, one in Pilsen, and one in Opava come to logically similar conclusions? Because this unspoken agreement is not there. Let us suppose that each town had at least one man, and these men observed our Czech life, and, thinking alike, came to similar conclusions, and worked in accordance with them. These men would form an unconscious, unorganized association of the greatest importance. It does not exist. We lack the political discussions of other nations, especially the large ones; for instance, the Germans show a great consensus of opinion in aims and tendencies, manifesting itself in various ways, giving them national strength, and endangering such nations as lack it.

As concerns tactics, our primary object is not to decide whether we should proceed more or less towards the left, but rather whether or not we are right; only then, on the basis of our true and right judgment, should we determine what procedure to take, according to our beliefs and temperaments. We should allow neither clubs nor political parties nor anything else to suppress our beliefs. We should resist the spirit of compromise which prevails all over Bohemia. We may remark yet again to-day that there is but little difference between these with the most extreme tendencies on either side. I believe that even the most ardent partisan will agree with opposing factions on many points, if they have the same objectives and if they are sufficiently educated to become aware of what they are, and to discover the means of reaching them. Then there may be a certain kind of co-operation between the factions. In every politically educated nation we see that the most extremely opposed parties sometimes work for each other, that every party man knows when his adversary will serve his aim, and that consequently amid the greatest strife there is a certain bond, a certain limit which no foe will overstep. This again postulates that tacit accord which I mentioned above. Fidelity does not depend upon stagnation, but is based upon independent agreement.

21. *Concerning Compromise*

The subject of compromise would require many words. I should like to call attention to Morley's work on the subject. Every compromise is bad. The question is whether it affects principle or only indifferent matters. If principle is endangered, compromise is morally impossible. We know from experience that very few occasions arise in which indifferent matters only are at stake. Compromise, therefore, most frequently means that in principle the party to it gave in; thus originates the ethical and political dilettantism so common in our country. The voters will pass a radical resolution as readily as, within the hour, they will pass a conservative one; I do not hold the electoral masses responsible. The man from the country does not understand politics, he is not very much interested in these matters, having heard only a few formal political speeches in all his life. But it is just the intellectuals who should

be blamed: the onus falls upon the comparatively small class of educated people.

Thus, if a new and better order of things is
to replace the old we must all bring it about
by studying politics properly and by showing
a stronger determination to stand for our truth,
by cultivating a fearlessness in speaking our
minds, far greater than exists to-day. Let us
not flatter the nation and let us not say that
the nation desires this, the nation wishes that.
Simple honesty requires that the relation of
the individual to the whole should be different
from what it is to-day.

BIBLIOGRAPHY

(As given by author)

KRAEPELIN, EMIL: *Zur Hygiene der Arbeit,* 1896.

KRAEPELIN, EMIL: *Über geistige Arbeit,* 1894.

BÜCHER, KARL: *Arbeit und Rhythmus,* 1896.

MOSSO, ANGELO: *Die Ermüdung* (deutsch von Glinzer), 1892.